REAL WOMEN

Eat Chiles

by Jane Butel

Food photography by
Christopher Marchetti

NORTHLAND PUBLISHING

www.northlandbooks.com

Composed in the United States of America
Printed in China

Edited by Claudine J. Randazzo
Designed by Katie Jennings
Cover Photograph by John Running
Index compiled by Jan Williams, Indexing Services

FIRST IMPRESSION 2006
ISBN 10: 0-87358-897-5
ISBN 13: 978-0-87358-897-3

06   07   08   09   10   5   4   3   2   1

Library of Congress Cataloging-in-Publication Data
Butel, Jane
Real women eat chiles / Jane Butel ; photography by Christopher Marchetti.
p. cm.
Includes index.
1. Cookery (Peppers) 2. Cookery (Hot peppers) 3. Low-calorie diet – Recipes. I. Title
TX803.P46B88 2006
641.3'384—dc22
2005055504

This book
is dedicated to my mother,
who always loved chiles of all sorts,
and to the real women everywhere
who love chile.

—J.B.

Contents

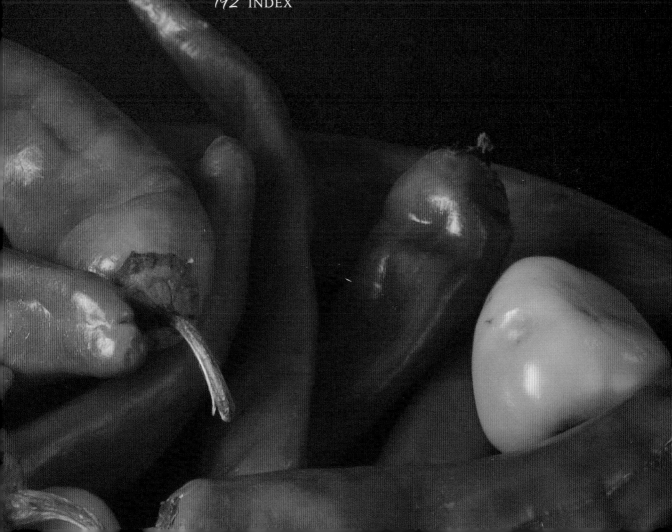

The Chile Parade

I am frequently asked, "How do you stay lean and in shape being around food all the time?" I credit my love of chiles. I include chiles quite liberally in my diet, eating them almost every day in one form or another. I am also dedicated to exercise and eating a balanced diet including lots of whole grains and fresh fruits and vegetables, which is easy because they are all highly complemented by chiles.

The real secret is that spicy, flavorful food pleasantly fills one up, and it can be adapted to one's food preferences and lifestyle. Eating a distorted diet where the food groups are unbalanced and the foods are often not that flavorful will only lead to quick weight gain when one returns to normal eating patterns.

Perhaps rapid weight loss is the immediate benefit of "fad" diets, but the lowered weight cannot be sustained, as the diet is just plain boring and in some cases not good for overall health. The real answer is to develop a desire for hot and spicy foods; find out what kinds and types of chiles you like, and incorporate them as much as possible into a healthy, balanced diet. My goal in writing this book is to show health-conscious people how chiles do so many good things for our bodies. I am constantly amazed. In addition to helping control the desire to overeat, chiles help our bodies burn calories. And, chiles offer that exciting endorphin rush as well. Really, what more could one want?

Through the years, I have made it a lifelong quest to search for chiles—first to understand them and research how they "work" and then to learn how populations from as long ago as the Egyptians and ancients in America and Asia sought them out and relished them. This book brings my decades of experiences with chiles together in a tangible and exciting way. I'll introduce you to real women who are fit and healthy and love chiles as I do, as well as offer quick-and-easy recipes that will liven up any diet and contribute to a better lifestyle.

I have had a lifelong love affair with chiles! My childhood memories surrounding chiles are many. I remember my father and I watching my Uncle Harry eat whole, pickled jalapeños out of cans he got from Mexico and finding the courage to eat them myself. I remember the thrill of picking chiles right out of the garden and teasing my friends with the biting sting they would get when I encouraged them to touch the inside of one.

I can also remember eating so much chili con carne as a young teenager that I felt sick. Any which way I could get that chile flavor has always appealed to me. I had to learn to monitor myself, however, a lesson that has helped me maintain my health and weight throughout my lifetime.

I have often reflected on just why I love chiles so much. I think it all started with my parents, as so many things do. My mother was born in Corpus Christi, Texas, and raised with a lot of influence from her Mexican nannies. She always loved Mexican food, especially a good, homemade tamale—the

1

kind made with red chile-laden beef filling in a fluffy white masa crust. She also liked chili con carne, enchiladas, and spicy food in general—which was so different than my girlfriends' mothers, especially in rural north-eastern Kansas. While most families around us were sitting down to the daily, traditional Midwest supper, my family was growing chiles on our farm and cooking up all sorts of innovative chile dishes in our country kitchen. Ours was an adventurous kitchen where something interesting was always bubbling in the pot!

My father loved hot stuff too. He liked to liberally sprinkle whatever form of chiles he could find on most all the sauces, gravies, and dishes he prepared. I can remember an unusual family favorite he often made on Sunday mornings. It was a very spicy, meaty gravy that he served with buckwheat pancakes. As unusual as it sounds, it was delicious!

Uncle Harry also had a major influence on my developing passion for chiles. He worked and lived in Mexico for many years, directing a large joint program with the American and Mexican governments. While there, he married a Mexican woman who had very refined taste. Because of her, we had the pleasure of many wonderful spice-laden meals.

I always like to say that every man, woman, and child in my family loved to cook, with the exception of my mother's father. My mother and maternal grandmother were both graduate Home Economists, although at the turn of the twentieth century, when my grandmother got her degree, Home Economics was called Domestic Science. My father liked to both grow most every kind of foodstuff as well as cook it—and almost always with chiles. He was a highly-regarded Agricultural Economist and taught all manner of farming from soil conservation to animal husbandry. He was even the head judge at the American Royal in Kansas City, one of the largest cattle shows in the world. Growing and preparing food was serious business in my family.

My love affair with chiles continued to develop in high school, where I was always the designated cook to prepare large vats of chili con carne that was a favorite at fundraisers for our school and church activities. It seemed that no matter where I was, I some-how wound up as the cook. One particular summer, between my sophomore and junior years in college, my life-long girl friend, Janet Beers, and I decided to rent a house that we shared with three other girlfriends. We were always throwing parties and my favorite specialties in those days were making spicy,

"While leading the first ascent of Mt. Everest with a disabled climber, I learned to make a chile concoction of ground, dried red chiles, garlic, salt, and water that the Sherpas used as a seasoning. They call it "Sherpa oxygen." It really energizes the taste buds, clears out the sinuses, and enables you to breathe better. I still use it on climbing expeditions because it is a lightweight paste that really packs a punch."

—*Angela Hawse,*
AMGA CERTIFIED ROCK GUIDE,
& HER DOG CHILE

homemade pizza and spaghetti sauce. I always made sure ample crushed red chile was added to each for that extra bite and zing.

Upon graduating from college with a degree in Home Economics and Journalism, I started working as a Home Economist for Public Service Co. of New Mexico, an investor-owned electric utility. (It has grown greatly since.) When I joined the department, they were really struggling and had very little programming. Within a year, I was appointed the head of the department, although I was only twenty-two years old. Now I had my chance!

To me, the obvious next step was to start teaching adult classes on the local, traditional dishes that are so unique to New Mexico. It was an instant success! In no time, we started filling each auditorium in the towns we served, from Deming near the Mexican border to Las Vegas, New Mexico, close to Colorado. Now I was really cooking with chiles, all kinds and both red and green. Our customers loved learning how to parch, peel, and stuff the large New Mexico green chiles to make chiles rellenos and how to make red and green chile sauces for enchiladas and most any Mexican-type dish.

I have always been proud of the attention our programming garnered. I won seven national awards in ten years and was then

selected to head the Home Economics Department for Con Edison in New York City, soon to be called the Department of Consumer Affairs.

By that time I had tested, developed, and written many, many chile recipes. I wrote two cookbooks and had the manuscript started for a comprehensive Southwest regional cookbook. Suddenly chiles had become more than just a personal culinary favorite in my life; they were now an integral component of my career. In fact, when we moved from New Mexico to New York, the moving men even noticed. As they packed the truck with fifty pounds of ground red chile, cases of canned green chiles, blue corn meal, corn masa, and corn husks, they commented, "You don't want to leave very badly, do you?"

After settling into life in New York City, my friends and acquaintances all came to know that I cooked with chiles, and they begged me to cook for them. To get fresh chiles for chiles rellenos and the like, I even tried growing green chile and contacted the New Mexico State Department of Agriculture Chile Specialist, Jim Nakiyama, who was a great friend, to get the seeds; but they did not do well in the soggy Long Island climate. They blossomed profusely, but the fruit was all stubby and often mildewed inside. To grow well, chiles need sandy soil, bright sun, and not too much water—the opposite of the growing conditions there.

I found myself really missing those hot chile flavors that were so abundant in New

"I am definitely a green chile fanatic—it's a staple in my kitchen! I use it wherever I can on whatever I can. Green chile adds the unique color and flavor of New Mexico to virtually any food. It's addictive!"

—Barbara Richardson
FIRST LADY OF NEW MEXICO

Mexico. I cooked them every chance I could. There was never a shortage of friends and acquaintances who liked to eat my spicy fare. I tended to specialize in traditional New Mexican dishes such as the red chile beef enchiladas, rellenos, burritos, carne adobado, and the like. As often as possible, I liked to also serve chunky guacamole—not the green gooey puree so frequently served back then. Sopaipillas were always a hit. I taught Amy, my only child, to fry them when she was three years old, so that I could have perfectly puffed and hot ones to accompany those meals.

Periodically during my corporate career, major manufacturers of Mexican foods asked me to consult with recipe development, chile marketing, and other related projects. I developed recipes for the cans of Mexican foods in the Old El Paso line that Pet. Inc. had just acquired, even though I was working for Public Service Co. While at General Electric, after Heublien acquired Ortega brand chiles, upon request, I created a cookbook using their products and assisted with marketing.

And while living in New York City, I was frequently asked to be part of Mexican food promotions at department stores along with James Beard and other famous foodies. I never really knew who kept recommending me for the "chile jobs," but I definitely felt a "calling."

I was on the corporate fast-track, eventually landing the position of Corporate Vice President for Consumer Affairs and Marketing for American Express, which was the first corporate officer position AMEX had ever awarded to a woman. However, during this time I was constantly being tugged and pulled by foodie friends to join the parade. I was continuously told that someone of my background was needed in this blossoming world of food development. So I did. I left the corporate world behind and joined the chile parade. I started writing, developing recipes, teaching, and even created a chile company, Pecos Valley Spice Co. It was a tough decision, but the yearning for food and developing a "spicy career" overcame me, and I've never looked back.

You, too, can benefit from the healthy fun of "sparking" your food with chiles. Read on...I am sure you will be totally amazed at the health benefits of chiles as well as their intriguing history. This fun food has actually been a favorite of the ancients across the world. Don't wait any longer to grab for the chiles and join the chile parade!

"These women grew up using chiles; they were literally a part of every meal. Their book, Secrets of Salsa, *came out of a classroom activity to help them learn English through sharing their salsa recipes. The salsa is, in a sense, an excuse for empowering the women and giving them independent lives."*

—*Barbara Goodell,*
COORDINATOR OF ANDERSON VALLEY ADULT SCHOOL
The "Salsitas" (pictured are Laura Morales, left; Maria Elena Plancarte, middle; Evangelina Angulo, right)

More Than the Common Fruit

THE ORIGIN OF CHILES

A visit to the Louvre in Paris a few years ago led me to the most interesting, and rather shocking, discovery. An ancient Egyptian mummy (as I recall the mummy was from a few thousand years BC and a female) had been buried with several dried whole red chiles. It was an intriguing sight, and I wondered how the chiles got to Egypt so long ago? Some proposed theories are that South America was attached to Africa and perhaps the chiles spread to Africa before the "great divide." Another theory is that chiles were a favorite with the slave traders from long, long ago. The ancients did discover the wonderful "keeping" or anti-oxidative quality chiles possess and used them for meat preservation. Key examples are "jerk" meats, such as Jamaican jerk pork or chicken and carne adobado, a popular dish in Hispanic America. In either dish, the red chiles are used to preserve the meat.

Another observation of the very early use of chiles, though not as old as the Egyptian mummy, was a display of chiles in the Natural History Museum in New York City that were found among pottery chards in a South American burial cave from pre-Biblical times.

I have learned that no one really knows for sure where chiles specifically originated, but they did evolve in the Americas—somewhere in South America and most likely in Peru. Many think they evolved as much smaller fruit and through cultivation were expanded into many different varieties and heats. There are more than seven thousand recorded varieties of chiles. They are part of the large nightshade family, which contains many fruits and vegetables, including tomatoes, potatoes, and eggplant. Chiles are classified as a fruit.

Ancient traders of all sorts evidently discovered the happy qualities of chiles and spread them around the world. Chiles, particularly the hot, feisty ones, grow easily almost everywhere. The larger chiles, such as those developed initially in Old Mexico and more recently, since World War II, in New Mexico, seem more specific to sandy soil, hot sun, and limited water.

In China, chiles were so revered in the populated areas of the mainland that it was not until the Communist takeover in the mid-twentieth century that chiles were allowed to be consumed as food. Prior, chiles were strictly reserved as a pharmaceutical. They were used to treat stomach ailments, cure ulcers, purify the blood, reduce arthritic pain, and many other uses. An interesting aside is that chiles were never forbidden in the Mongolian desert, as it was impossible to police their use among the nomadic tribes that developed the spicy Chinese foods such as Szechwan and Hunan. Most anthropologists explain that American Indians west of the Mississippi can trace their genetics and inherited DNA from the Mongolian and Tibetan populations. So if the Mongolians and Tibetans were among the first to explore and inhabit the western areas of the Americas, coming across the Bering Strait, it would have been quite natural for them to bring chiles back to Asia, explaining how chiles got to the Asian continent.

The American Indians also valued chiles because of their amazing keeping or antioxidative qualities. They sprinkled chiles on meats before drying them into jerky to extend their keeping quality. (I have always thought stewing the jerky to make it more easily eaten was the beginning of our popular American chili or chili con carne.) I guess chiles can be thought of as a kind of substitute for refrigeration, to some extent. Of course, American Indians had other options for preserving foods as well, such as drying, smoking, and salting.

Perhaps the generous use of very hot chiles in India is the most difficult to explain. India is a large, ancient population, where very sophisticated dishes are made with a range of chiles, all hot. The research I have done yields that chiles in India were probably introduced by Marco Polo. However, I think they more than likely arrived there much sooner. So many wonderfully spicy dishes in India impress me with the fact that they had a very ancient development.

CURATIVE PROPERTIES

The healthful properties of chiles have long been known with the ancients and those practicing homeopathy. An amazingly large number of chile cures are related by Dr. John Heinerman, Ph.D. in his book, *The Health Benefits of Cayenne* (Keats Publishing Inc., 1999). A specific example he attributes to chiles is as a cure for congestive heart failure. One notable case is of a fairly young man of forty-two years of age who suffered a near-fatal heart attack, blocking ninety-eight percent of the main artery leading to the heart. He underwent major bypass surgery, followed by a restrictive no-fat diet. Six months later, he suffered the symptoms of congestive heart failure and decided not to accept prescribed medications. He researched possible cures and decided to try capsaicin, the potent compound found in chiles, and started taking three pills daily with his meals. Some eighteen years later, he was "good as new." I often share my own personal explanation of this to the students I teach at the cooking school, which is that chiles act like Drano in our vascular system, augering out plaque that clogs our arteries.

"As a professional mountain bike racer I thrive on adrenalin. I love the rush I get from descending a gnarly trail or climbing uphill and pushing my physical limits. At home, I like to add chiles to my food to help achieve that same feeling."

—Dara Marks-Marino
PROFESSIONAL MOUNTAIN BIKE RACER

Heinerman's book details cures for itching, mouth sores, kidney problems, and the flu, among many others. The kidney cure got my attention as I was born with one malfunctioning kidney (and one very good one). For the kidney cure, he relates that DeWitt Clinton Pendery, the founder of Pendery's spices back in 1870 in Fort Worth, Texas, developed a blend of cayenne pepper, cumin, and oregano that was popular with local doctors, as it helped inactive kidneys, alleviated pain accompanying kidney stones, as well as stimulated the lymph glands, producing more beautiful-looking skin.

The cure for influenza Heinerman related was interesting in that it came from a Mayan *curandera* or medicine woman. It was a combination of the local sour orange juice and a pinch of cayenne. This was drunk and gargled and cured the flu symptoms in twenty-four hours!

Loving raw oysters and all manner of seafood, cooked or raw, my eyes darted to the section on how scientists at the October 1993 meeting of the American Society for Microbiology, at Louisiana State University Medical Center, conducted a series of tests with certain noxious bacteria obtained from spoiled, raw seafood. When cayenne was added as in straight hot sauce, all the bacteria were killed. No wonder I love lots of Tabasco® or any really hot sauce whenever I eat raw oysters! In the testing, it was found that lemon juice and horseradish also helped reduce the bacteria but not as completely as the hot sauce. So if you are like me and enjoy the combination of all of the above, it seems there is a really good reason to keep adding the hot sauce.

The cures and healthful properties of chiles that are continuously discovered are amazing. According to Dr. Reuben Lotan of the University of Texas M.D. Anderson Cancer Center in Houston, "Capsaicin can prevent cancer development in animal models and cause cancer cell death in cultured tumor cells." (Reuters Health, © 2005.) In simple language, the cancer cells were starved of oxygen, even in carcinomas, due to capsaicin.

Chile research is continuing, such as for the treatment of diabetic neuropathy or nerve pain. Topical capsaicin is helpful to those suffering with diabetes because it inhibits substance P, an amino acid peptide associated with pain. Another benefit to diabetics Heinerman also related is that capsaicin has the effect of lowering blood sugar.

"People often ask me what I put chiles in, besides salsa. My response is always, 'What wouldn't you put chiles in?' Chiles are great in desserts, soups, breads, as well as main dishes. Chiles are a daily part of our cuisine. A day without chiles would be dull, for all of the senses. And the crop is as beautiful to grow as it is delicious!"

—Susan Welsand, "THE CHILE WOMAN"

The helpful effects of chiles in the entire digestive track are numerous—from cauterizing ulcers to aiding in overall digestion. As reported in the *Nutrition Reporter* ("Hot Peppers Lead to Even Hotter Research on Arthritis and Other Conditions", © 1995), by Jack Challem, "People suffering from ulcers are usually warned to avoid spicy foods. But new research suggests that capsaicin is the opposite—that capsaicin might actually protect against peptic ulcers." In fact in studies over the years, it has been found that capsaicin protects the gastric mucosal membrane against damage from alcohol and aspirin.

In the same article, Jin Y. Kang, MD of the National University of Singapore, speculated that capsaicin might work by stimulating a hormone that increases blood flow and nourishes the gastric mucosal membrane and that spicy food in general might be helpful. Knowing that the Chinese in mainland China were forbidden to have chiles in their diet until Mao Tsa Tung took over, it is interesting to note the fact that mainland Chinese have far more peptic ulcers than Chinese who were not restricted against eating chiles. "Kang discovered that ulcer-free patients ate 2.6 times more chile than those with ulcers. The ulcer-free patients also ate chile more often—24 times per month, compared with 8 times per month for those with ulcers."

The history of chiles and their effect on the blood have long been known. Those who eat a diet with generous amounts of chiles, such as in Thailand, have a much lower incidence of blood clotting disease. Research definitively indicates that upon searching the medical records of countries where spicy foods are regularly consumed, that people who eat a diet high in red peppers experience a much lower incidence of blood clotting diseases. In summary, chiles reduce hypertension, increase the pulse, and help stem off strokes and the ravishing effects of high blood pressure.

Externally, capsaicin produces burn-like symptoms on people with great sensitivity. The good news is that with most people the burning goes away after repeated exposures to chiles. This burning sensation can have very positive healing properties in the arthritic. The application of capsaicin creams decreases pain in the joints caused by arthritis and actually arrests the destruction of cartilage. It acts to stop the breaking down of fluid in the joints. Physiologically, capsaicin creams and ointments penetrate to the arthritic joints and stop the destruction of synovial fluid. It is this destruction, or drying out, of joints that comes with aging that the capsaicin can actually reverse. External application of capsaicin creams can also control the pain associated with herpes, shingles, and the neuralgia and pain from amputation trauma.

"Grandpa says, '¡Gracias a Dios que chile is the world's most perfect food!'"

—Gloria Aguiñago and
Lisa Aguiñago-Mansfield
RESTAURANT OWNERS

Chiles actually make our bodies more efficient. They enhance the body's ability to digest fats, by decreasing the absorption of cholesterol and enhancing the liver's production of enzymes, reducing the storage of triglycerides. Chiles synergize with exercise, meaning with exercise they enhance the body's oxygen consumption rate. In simple terms, chiles increase one's metabolism, thus enhancing the opportunity to reduce and maintain a desirable weight.

Capsaicin produces an endorphin rush in our bodies in direct proportion to the heat units of the chiles. In other words, the hotter the chiles, the greater the reaction. An endorphin rush can be equated with an adrenalin rush or a "high." This is the internal reaction. This benefit is explained in more detail in "The Chile Habit" section of this book.

I ask, how can one not want to eat chiles? I am actually sensitive to really hot chiles that produce pain and no pleasure. But I adore a hot and spicy dish, where the chiles are in good balance with acidic ingredients. Acids are the key to capsaicin control. In fact, when cooking a dish with a great number of chiles in it, such as the Basic Red Chile Sauce (page 164), it is important to check the chiles you will be using in the preparation of the dish. If they are painfully hot to you, then calm them down with an acidic ingredient, such as tomato or lime juice, wine, or vinegar. Sprinkling freshly squeezed lime juice over too hot chiles can make a noticeable difference. In Mexico, this is a frequent practice for dishes such as chiles rellenos, which are stuffed chiles. Since chiles are the primary ingredient, they must be of an agreeable heat level so people can eat them. In Old Mexico, generally they do not like dishes as hot as they do in New Mexico—explaining in part why they marinate their rellenos chiles in lime juice. In New Mexico, they do not.

With medical research focused on the cure for cancer and how stress increases cancer risk, it is good to understand the practical and very useful information about how the regular consumption of chiles can have an effect of bracing one's body against all the ravages of stress. Knowing that, overall, chiles work so many healthy wonders in our bodies, why not enjoy them as I do?

"To my enjoyment, I have encountered pleasant surprises in local spice wherever I have traveled throughout the world. It is wonderful to find chile in so many places."

—*Dr. Beth Claxton,*
OBSTETRICIAN & GYNECOLOGIST

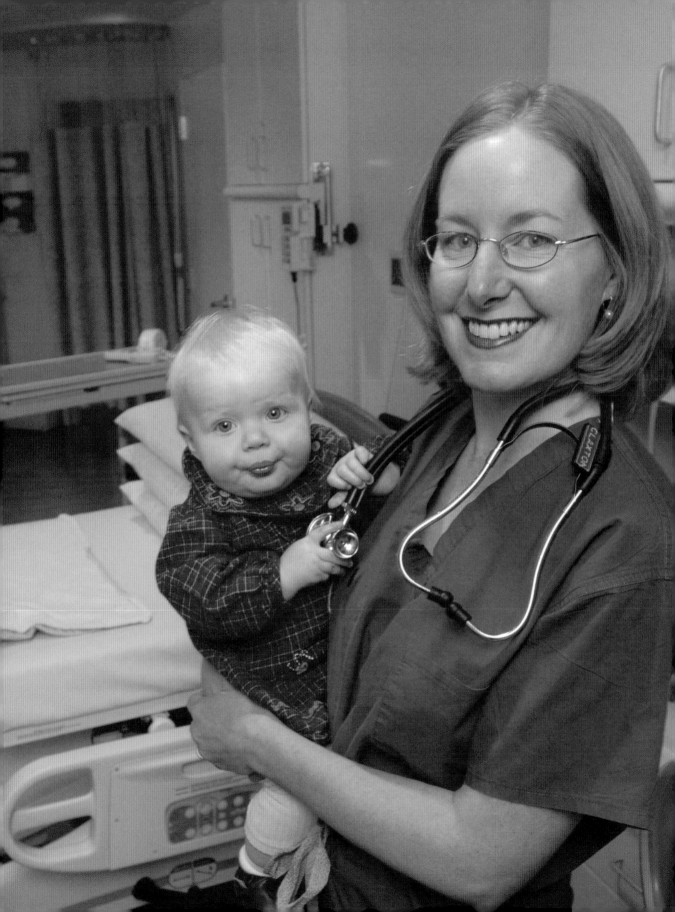

PART TWO

The Chile Habit

HOW CHILES CAN ADD SPICE
TO YOUR LIFE & BODY

Chiles are unique in so many ways—the most important being their possession of capsaicin—an amazing stimulant that has other properties as well. Capsaicin is an oil born acid possessing very strong, burning properties in the hottest of chiles. A great deal of the stimulation that capsaicin provides in our bodies can be credited to capsaicin producing an endorphin rush in direct proportion to the heat units of the chiles. An endorphin rush or a "high" is an internal reaction. In other words, the hotter the chile, the more capsaicin, the better it is for you, and the better it makes you feel! Capsaicin intensity is what cures.

Endorphins were discovered only thirty years ago, in 1975, by John Hughes and Hans Kosterlitz in the brain of a pig. Endorphins are opiod neuropeptides, and they produce a morphine-like reaction in our bodies. The word comes from endogenous morphine or Greek for cerebrum. Endorphins are produced by the pituitary gland and the hypothalamus in vertebrates and are then released in the body. They resemble opiates in that they work as natural pain killers. They regulate one's mood, relieve pain and hunger, assist memory, reduce aging by removing superoxides, and are even connected to the production of sex hormones.

In sum, endorphins are natural morphine receptors. These receptors are anti-stress hormones that relieve pain naturally. The more technical definition is that endorphins are a small chain of peptides that actuate opiate receptors, producing a feeling of well-being. Twenty different types of endorphins have been discovered in the nervous system. There are four main types of endorphins: alpha, beta, gamma, and sigma. The most effective endorphin is the beta-endorphin, which gives the most euphoric effect to the brain; it is composed of thirty-one amino acids.

Amazingly, chile is one of the primary producers of endorphin reactions that are not created by physical movement. Chocolate is also. No wonder I love the combination of chile and chocolate, such as in the Spicy Hot Chocolate Mousse on page 189. Other producers of endorphin reactions are all physical— exercise, acupuncture, yoga, laughter, sex, etc. The overall benefit of endorphin production is its reduction of the ravaging effects of stress, pain, suppression of hunger, increased memory, and a sense of well-being.

Specifically, getting a "runner's high" or a "second wind" or the blissful feelings one gets after sex are related to increased endorphin production. Since chiles are one of the primary producers of endorphin reactions that can be consumed, why not find your very own way to unfold this pleasure source? With the healthful properties of chiles, the main challenge to the

THE CHILE HABIT 21

uninitiated is just discovering the tastes and recipes that are pleasurable and the levels that are most pleasing. Be aware, that the more hot stuff you eat, the more you will crave it—coming full circle to the fact that chiles are about the best food that you can eat. There is simply no way you will hurt yourself unless you have a particular allergic or sensitivity that would inhibit you.

As I mentioned earlier, eating chiles actually stimulates the use of oxygen in the body—especially when paired with exercise. Exercising early in the day is thought to be the best preparation for an overall sense of well-being all day long. And, your body operates more efficiently, making it easier to maintain or lose weight.

Each one of us is an individual with an individual palate. What is stimulating to one person may just barely be spicy to another. Since chiles are addictive, the more you eat them, the more you will want to eat them, and the hotter you will desire them to be. Those of us who have been "exposed" to chiles early in life, such as I, are constantly on a quest for a daily chile fix. Those who have not had the opportunity to eat chiles have much less tolerance for capsaicin. However, it is never too late to start a daily habit of chile eating and develop one's own "chile drive."

Adding the spice of chiles to our diets allows us to have total freedom of diet. Of course, each of us should be aware of what is best for us individually. Eating fruits, vegetables, whole grains, and proteins is always important. In other words, eat a balanced diet. With chile added to your daily diet, you have literally a whole world of spicy cuisines from which to select in addition to southwestern. This book offers some of the best tested, quick-and-easy southwestern chile-laden recipes from which you can choose for your own meal planning. You will soon find that the high and excitement from eating chiles is so much fun and supplies such a great sense of well-being that you will probably be wondering "why didn't I know this before?"

The most enforceable diet or lifestyle is one that eliminates the feeling of being controlled or consumed by too many hard to follow or, worse yet, boring rules. Formulated diets or fad diets are appealing because of their promise. But when one goes off the diet, most often the weight creeps right back. What really works is a change in habits or lifestyle if one truly wants to be a leaner, healthier person. With generous portions of chile on a regular basis, you can create the recipes and eat the foods that feature your favorite flavors. And there are so many chiles to choose from—some say more than seven thousand varieties—and so many preparations. You

"A day without chile is a day without sunshine!"

— Sara Moulton

EXECUTIVE CHEF FOR *GOURMET* MAGAZINE;
FOOD EDITOR OF *GOOD MORNING AMERICA*;
HOST OF *SARA'S SECRETS* ON THE FOOD NETWORK

just can never get bored with chiles amply sprinkled throughout your foods. And, you will be a leaner, healthier YOU! To say nothing of all the healthful side benefits supplied by endorphins.

For example, I have a friend, Wendy, who has worked with me for many years in my cooking school on a periodic basis as a volunteer and sometimes a regular employee. Wendy likes food and food likes Wendy, meaning she is almost always trying one diet or another. She is never able to completely stay on a diet long enough to really lose considerable pounds and if she does, the pounds come right back after she is no longer on the diet. She claims one of her most successful diets for getting off a few pounds quickly is to make the Chicken Tortilla Chowder on page 130 and keep the soup in the refrigerator. Instead of varied dinners, she will have the chowder every night for a week. To me, the monotony of eating the same food for a week does not appeal. For Wendy, it works.

Once you get the chile habit, which is such a healthy addiction, you can choose from a wide range of foods that suit your taste. You can use chile as an ingredient, such as in the Aztec Pork Chops on page 62. Or you can place the chiles in a salsa, rub, sauce, compound butter, or just sprinkle it over the top of any dish. What is really fun is using your imagination to create your very own recipes using the recipes that follow in the next section as a guide.

After your body gets adjusted to being happily stimulated daily with a balanced, spicy diet complemented with your favorite exercise, you will have developed the most sustaining lifestyle, and one that you can live with the rest of your life. And you will be lean. I have always loved to cook and create new recipes, and ones with chiles are particularly appealing. The more I research about chiles the more I am certain that they have been my sustaining force through the stresses dealt my way. I am often asked how I can look so trim, have such good skin, and be in apparent good health at my age with all the stresses I have had. I honestly feel chiles share in that responsibility along with a love of yoga, exercise, massage, and being outdoors.

REAL WOMEN, & MEN, WHO EAT CHILES

Many others share my love of chiles. When I contacted Sara Moulton, Executive Chef with *Gourmet* magazine, host of *Sara's Secrets* on the Food Network, and the Food Editor of *Good Morning America*, she said she absolutely loves chiles, the hotter the better.

"Subtle or peppery, chiles contribute gustatory color to a meal. Similar to the way I overlay opaque and sheer fabrics to create my artworks, I try to layer the flavors of chiles to create complex, contrasting, and complementary tastes in a dish."

—Darcy Falk,
TEXTILE ARTIST

"As a teacher of mostly Mexican-American students and second-language learners, I have made chiles a part of my classroom. Since most of my students are so familiar with chiles, we read books about chiles to build their English vocabulary. We study the Columbian Exchange where chiles were taken back to Europe by Columbus and other explorers. But best of all, I have the privilege to sample many delicious foods containing chiles at class celebrations."

—*Bethanne Guertin Sally*
ELEMENTARY SCHOOL TEACHER

As we were talking, she had just sorted out the hot sauces in her refrigerator and found that she had thirty-five different varieties, ultimately weeding them down to just seventeen. And, she said, "A Day without chile is a day without sunshine! However, I try not to put chile in everything."

Barbara Richardson, the wife of governor of New Mexico Bill Richardson, says, "I am definitely a green chile fanatic—it's a staple in my kitchen! I use it wherever I can on whatever I can. Green chile adds the unique color and flavor of New Mexico to virtually any food. It's addictive!"

Recently, Dr. Virginia Barlow, a medical doctor, attended our weekend cooking school in Albuquerque, New Mexico. Hailing from Coudersport, Pennsylvania, her magnetic personality attracted me immediately. I was impressed with how much she really and truly loved chiles and also with her great knowledge about their curative qualities. When I invited her to make a contribution to this book, she wrote the following:

"Chile is the spice of life, and without it, we women would all be sickeningly sweet (and boring). We need to spice things up every once in a while. That's why eating chile is a way of life for me. It's what gives me that extra zip, zest, and pizzazz!

"Also, let's not forget the amazing health benefits derived from eating chiles. It's hard to imagine, but it's true; by eating those hot little ol' chile peppers everyday, you will improve your immune system, prevent heart disease by lowering cholesterol, and promote weight loss. Chiles are also an excellent source of vitamin A, which is a potent antioxidant. So by incorporating chiles into your daily diet, not only will you be protecting yourself from developing cancer, you will also enjoy the added benefit of slowing the aging process.

"What's my favorite way to eat chiles? Well, let's see…there's chile tea, chile ice cream, and green chile pork stew. Of course, there's the dish everyone is most familiar with…chili. But my all-time favorite chile dish is chile cheese grits. (A quick version of this recipe is on page 155.) Amazing, isn't it? Who would have ever thought that spicing things up would actually be good for you?"

When I think of famous women known for their chile love, I always think of Elizabeth Taylor, who became known for her love of chili while filming *Cleopatra*. She would have generous amounts of Dave Chasen's famous chili frozen and air shipped to her weekly from his prestigious restaurant in Hollywood.

Years ago, predating the *Oprah Winfrey Show*, there was a particular instance when I was cooking a green chile sauce for enchiladas on the *People are Talking* television show, which broadcast from Baltimore, Maryland. At the time, Oprah Winfrey was the host. She was completely fascinated with the chiles I was using and asked me to create a special green chile enchilada using Maryland crab.

I did, and she absolutely loved it! In fact she invited me back to do two more chile shows.

Another time, when I was touring my original Tex-Mex cookbook, back in 1980, I was a guest on the *Mike Douglas Show* along with Lee Marvin and Joey Bishop. I brought a pound tin each of my Pecos Valley hot and mild red chile as kind of a prop. Well, Joey got the bright idea to rub some of the red chile right on Lee's cheeks. Soon Lee was paying back Joey with the same treatment. To add to the antics, they asked me to make margaritas to accompany the chimichangas I was preparing. Of course I was ready and whipped it all up. The "chile rubbing" was the most memorable part of the show! It seems as though everyone likes chile.

Bo Derek, famous for her starring role in *Ten* has been personally ordering chile and spices from our spice company, Pecos Valley Spice Co., for years.

Closer to home, my daughter, Amy, was brought up on chiles and just loves them. When asked for her favorite dish, she could not come up with it—she said she just loves anything with green chile in it—but also likes red chile, just not as well. And my husband's mother, who lived to 102, had to have a daily chile fix. She grew up in west Texas and lived in Texas and New Mexico her entire life. If she didn't have enchiladas or the like, she drank a tea of hot red chile and vinegar every day.

At this point, you may be wondering about the different spellings for "chile." Long ago, I thought it best to call the beef-laden dish generously spiced with red chiles, "chili" and to call the fruit, "chile."

Knowing how healthy chiles are for you, I am sure you are wondering just how to include them in your diet without going to a lot of trouble and having to learn new ways to cook. For this purpose, I have selected some of my personal, easy-to-make recipes for this book. Each recipe averages only five ingredients and should be made in about twenty minutes or less. These should provide a guide for you to develop your own healthy chile recipes.

Try to have chiles at least once a day or prepare a chile tea made by bringing water to a boil and placing a tea infuser filled with crushed chiles into the boiling water. Turn the heat off and steep for about five minutes, then add honey to taste and about one tablespoon cider vinegar for each pint of hot tea. This tea can be made in quantity and refrigerated for those days when you just need the tea because you have not otherwise enjoyed chiles.

"Chile is like a religion here in New Mexico—we're weaned on it, we eat it raw and roasted, by itself, and with everything. On our small farm in the Sangre de Cristo Mountains outside of Taos, we grow garlic and other crops, but it's too cold here to grow much chile, which sometimes breaks my heart. I love to pickle our garlic with roasted green chile and put it in big jars for the winter."

– Kristen Davenport,
WRITER & FARMER

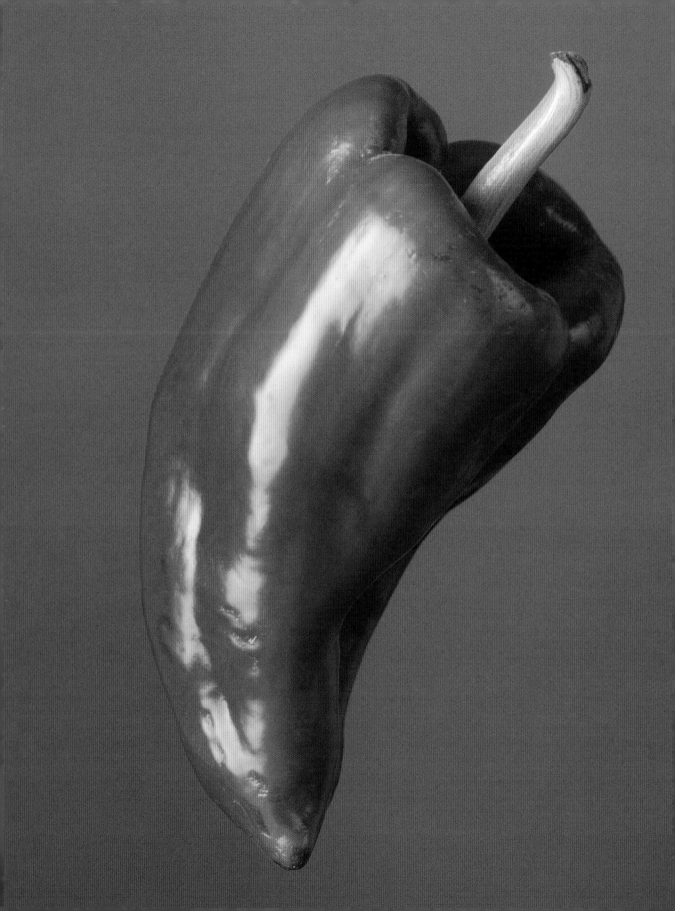

The Secrets of Cooking with Chiles

Chiles spark excitement into otherwise ho-hum dishes. Chiles add the most depth of flavor when they are used as an ingredient where the flavor is simmered or cooked into the food. When cooking with chiles, I always like to put in what I think will be enough to bring out a good flavor and then add more if needed at the end of the cooking period. If I am serving people whose food tastes I am unfamiliar with, I will put out a small bowl of hot chile, such as pequin or minced fresh jalapeño, with a tiny spoon alongside for individual adding—just like salt or pepper.

In New Mexico, the various Pueblo Indians make tiny votive bowls, about one to two inches in diameter out of pottery for feeding the spirits. They are perfect for placing ground chile in. In fact, I keep caribe and pequin chile in them at all times on my table. I had some wonderful Navajo women make me sterling salt cellar-size spoons with turquoise sets for serving the chiles, and it all makes for a fun and beautiful way to offer chile flavoring.

I use milder chiles for creating a flavor base, and add hotter ones for the desired heat. A sign of a good chile cook in New Mexico is that they do not use flour or meals of any kind to thicken sauces—they use milder chiles. Milder chiles have a starch-like quality that will thicken sauces and the like. Hotter chiles can be added to create the desired spiciness.

The spiciness of chiles within the palate replaces the desire for fatty, salty, or sugary foods that are less nutritious and higher in calories. I find that the addition of chiles balanced with some form of acid such as lime juice (a favorite), vinegar, or even wine, beer, or tequila will mellow or equalize the spiciness. With so many chiles to choose from, I am sure that after a bit of experimentation you will be able to find your favorites. One fact to keep in mind is that chiles are greatly influenced by their growing conditions, meaning that a single variety such as a New Mexico 604 may be just perfect for you most of the time and yet other times be too hot or mild. That is due to climactic factors—moisture, heat, soil, altitude, and the distance from the equator. I can remember my father telling me that he could recognize the difference between a chile grown north or south of Highway 66, now Interstate 40. Part of it is the latitude, but the other factor is the altitude. The higher the altitude, the hotter the chile. I will never forget the famous chile guru at New Mexico State, Dr. Jim Nakayama, who said that there could be up to thirty-five different piquancies on one plant at any one time. So, one must learn a bit of chile selection.

Fundamentally, the broader the shoulders and the blunter the tip for any one chile, the milder the chile will be. The reverse—the more sloping shoulders and pointed tip—make for a hotter chile. This holds true for both red and green chiles of any variety.

Admittedly, the rounder shaped ones such as the cascabel and the habanero do not have those determinants. Another interesting issue is that green chile, which is tremendously popular in New Mexico, is much less popular and available elsewhere. A green chile is a seasonal phenomenon and is basically an unripe red chile. In a green chile, the starches within the makeup of the chile are laden with vitamin C. Whereas when chiles ripen in October to become red, the starches change to sugars and are then rich with vitamin A—the sight vitamin, critical for seeing well in the dark. It does seem wondrous that the ripe red chiles with their abundant vitamin A needed for night sight are seasonally available, right when the vitamin is most needed with winter's longer nights.

Green chiles are generally always roasted or parched over or under direct heat to blister the tough skin. For best nutrition, flavor, and color, as soon as parched, they should be dunked in cold or ice water. My favorite way to keep the parched green chiles is to pat them dry after their cold water dunking, and freeze them on cookie sheets in the freezer,

making certain the chiles do not touch each other. When they are frozen rock solid, I bag them in freezer weight bags, labeling the date. Always use the older ones in the freezer first.

To use the frozen green chiles, rinse them under water and peel them immediately. The skin just slips right off. Then cut off the top inch and use the blunt side of the knife and run it along a stack of chiles, forcing out the seeds. Usually I just leave any seeds that are stubborn and do not slip out, but you can rinse them if desired. As a signature that I prepared the chile myself, rather than using commercially frozen or canned chiles, I always cut the chiles in ½- to 1-inch width pieces. I like these rather large pieces as you can really taste them, and I think they give a more attractive look to the sauces.

Red chiles can act as a substitute for black pepper and lime wedges a substitute for salt. The only factor is that the lime is perishable and must be continuously prepared—unlike salt which lasts until you use it.

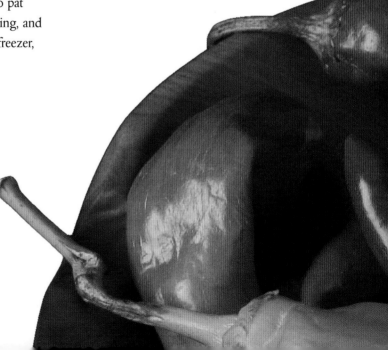

Red chiles are more perishable than you might think. Whether whole in pods or ground into powders, they will stay much fresher if refrigerated or frozen. When allowed to stay at room temperature, the oils become rancid, the color eventually fades—which is an indicator that the nutrition is also dissipating, and the flavor becomes stale due to rancidification of the oils. Refrigeration or freezing keeps the chiles fresh.

Whenever possible, I use powdered or crushed chiles as they are more dependable in their flavor, especially if they come from a source where the Scoville heat units are consistent. A British Scientist, Dr. Scoville, developed the Scoville heat units nearly a century ago. Essentially, the way it works is that the higher the heat unit attributed to the chile, the hotter it is. The way he assigned the units is that five thousand heat units is the line of demarcation between being a chile and a paprika. A chile must register five thousand heat units or more, and those are the mildest chiles. Habaneros or Scotch bonnets range all the way to two-hundred thousand units and are the most well known super hot chiles.

The best rule for cooking with chiles is that you can always add more if the flavor is not intense enough. Also be aware that adding less of a hot chile will not make a milder dish—it will still be hot, but have a weaker chile flavor. If mildness is sought, use mild chiles.

Have lots of fun with the following recipes. They are guides for dishes you can create using chiles. Each is healthy and quick to make, allowing you to include the many benefits of chile in creating your very own chile-laden dishes. Chiles add spark and excitement to eating, and your meals will be healthier and more flavorful.

Appetizers

A good place to start your chile diet is with appetizers!
Little bites of very flavorful spicy foods can do a
lot to diminish your appetite. The selection that
follows has recipes that are full of flavor, and
they can even supply a light meal when
accompanied by one of the soups, salads, or
wraps that are in the following chapters.

Guacamole

Fresh, fresh guacamole—made by dicing the avocado into half-inch dice and gently folding in the remaining ingredients—is so wonderful, and healthy too. Never substitute for the fresh ingredients. For ease in scooping out the avocado from the rind, try using an avocado gadget that pulls out the flesh and slices it into half-inch slices at the same time. Then follow the recipe, cutting the avocado with two table knives just enough to create the half-inch dice.

2 Hass avocados, soft when pressed with thumb

½ lime

1 clove garlic, minced

¼ cup tomato, chopped

¼ cup onion, chopped

1 jalapeño, minced

About ½ teaspoon salt (optional)

3 tablespoons cilantro, coarsely chopped (optional)

Slice the avocados in half and scoop out the flesh. Place in a medium bowl. Cut into half-inch dice, using two knives.

Squeeze some of the lime juice over the avocado. Add most of the tomato, onion, and jalapeño, reserving some if the avocados are small. Fold in carefully so as not to mash the avocado. Taste and adjust the seasoning, adding the salt, if desired. If needed for flavor, add the rest of the lime juice, tomato, onion, jalapeño, and cilantro (if using). Serve in an earthenware bowl with tostados or corn chips or fresh vegetable crudités.

Preparation time: 10 to 12 minutes, Yield: 4 servings

PER SERVING:
Calories 173
Protein 2 g
Carbohydrates 10 g
Fiber 5 g
Fat 16 g
Saturated Fat 2 g
Cholesterol 0 mg
Sodium 12 mg

Pinto Pâté

Generous chiles and chopped onion make the difference here between refried beans and this wonderful pâté! I like to use the hottest chiles that I and/or my guests like and place a small bowl of pickled jalapeños to the side for topping the pâté. Sliced or shredded cheese can also be added.

1 teaspoon extra-virgin olive oil, preferably Spanish

¼ cup onion, coarsely chopped

2 cloves garlic, coarsely chopped

2 cups pinto beans, cooked

¼ cup green chiles, chopped (2 fresh chiles, parched and peeled, or frozen or canned chiles)

Heat oil in a saucepan or skillet. Add the onion and garlic and sauté until they become clear and slightly browned.

Place the onion mixture, beans, and chiles in a food processor or blender and process until coarsely chopped. Return to the pan and heat until warm. Serve with Tortilla Toasts (page 36), use as a layer on Southwestern Pizzas (pages 111-113), or create nachos by spreading pâté on tostados and melting cheese on top of each.

Cooking Time: 5 to 6 minutes, Yield: 4 to 8 servings

PER SERVING:
(1/2 recipe)
Calories 70
Protein 4 g
Carbohydrates 13 g
Fiber 4 g
Fat 1 g
Saturated Fat 0 g,
Cholesterol 0 mg
Sodium 316 mg

Tortilla Toasts with Salsa-Marinated Mexican Caviar

These simple, quick-to-prepare toasts have a rich flavor and are enhanced with a sprinkle of your favorite "hot stuff." Save 25 calories of retained fat on average per tortilla or 6 calories per chip by baking instead of frying tortillas for dippers. Increase the flavor by spritzing with water containing a hint of oil (you can do this with a spritzer you fill yourself). Add seasoning mixes if desired to enhance the flavor. Chile is always good with a sprinkle of fresh lime juice.

8 corn tortillas (6-inch size)

Dust of your choice, such as Southwest seasoning salt or rub, ground pure red or green chile, dry southwestern salad dressing, or dip mix

1 cup garbanzos, well-drained

½ cup salsa, any type

½ lime, juiced

2 tablespoons cilantro, coarsely chopped

Preheat the oven to 425 degrees F. Place the tortillas on a cutting board and cut them into 4 to 6 pieces. Arrange evenly on 1 large or 2 medium baking sheets. Dip your fingertips into a small bowl of water and sprinkle the tortillas or spray with a mister. Place the tortillas in the oven and bake for 5 minutes. Turn each piece and bake for 5 minutes longer. Remove from the oven and lightly sprinkle with whatever seasoning you wish, or shake the pieces in a bag containing the seasoning. These chips are best served warm. Freeze any remaining for reheating and serving later.

Meanwhile, prepare the "caviar" by combining the garbanzos with the salsa and lime juice. Taste and adjust the seasonings. Stir in most of the cilantro, reserving some for garnish. Serve in a bowl on a platter with the Tortilla Toasts encircling the bowl. Top the "caviar" with the reserved cilantro.

Preparation Time: 10 minutes, Yield: 4 to 8 servings

PER SERVING:
(1/8 recipe)
Calories 95
Protein 4 g
Carbohydrates 19 g
Fiber 3 g
Fat 1 g
Saturated Fat 0 g
Cholesterol 0 mg
Sodium 134 mg

Nacho Crisps with Goat Cheese, Fruit, and Lime Salsa

Fruit and chile are natural complements and offer a refreshing substitute for all the cheesy, fat-filled appetizers so often served. A southwestern-spiced goat cheese adds a little something extra, if available.

8 corn tortillas

1 cup nectarines, peaches, pears, or any firm-fleshed fruit, chopped

2 scallions, including the tender green tops, minced

2 cloves garlic, minced

¼ cup lime juice, freshly squeezed (1 large or 2 small limes)

1 tablespoon or more crushed red chile (such as pequin)

4 ounces goat cheese or cream cheese

Preheat the oven to 425 degrees F. Stack the tortillas on a cutting board and cut into quarters. Arrange evenly on one large or two medium baking sheets. Bake for 5 minutes. Turn each piece and bake for another 5 minutes, or until crisp.

Meanwhile, prepare the salsa by combining the fruit, scallions, garlic, lime juice, and crushed chile. Remove the crisps from the oven and let cool. Spread each with the goat cheese and top with the salsa. Or serve the cheese and salsa in separate bowls and arrange the tortilla crisps around the edges so each person can spread their own.

Preparation Time: 10 to 12 minutes, Yield: 4 servings

PER SERVING:
Calories 217
Protein 9 g
Carbohydrates 31 g
Fiber 4 g
Fat 7 g
Saturated Fat 4 g
Cholesterol 13 mg
Sodium 189 mg
(Analyzed with nectarines.)

Black Bean and Goat Cheese Chalupitas

These are really a variation on nachos and are quite good even for a light meal. Adding a hot home-prepared salsa or a round of pickled jalapeño to each really makes them special.

24 tostados, purchased or homemade
1 1-pound can refried black beans
4 ounces (½ cup) goat cheese, preferably with southwestern flavorings added (see Note)
24 pickled jalapeño slices or ½ cup homemade hot salsa, any kind (see pages 168-175)

Preheat the broiler. Place the tostados on a baking sheet. Spread each with a layer of black beans, then the cheese, and top with jalapeño slices or salsa. Place under the broiler for 3 to 5 minutes, until lightly bubbled. Serve hot.

Note: To prepare the southwestern-flavored goat cheese, if it is not commercially available, add to the cheese 1 teaspoon ground, pure mild red chile, 1 clove garlic (minced), and a pinch of cumin; stir to blend. Cream cheese can be substituted for goat cheese.

Cooking Time: 3 to 5 minutes, Yield: 4 to 6 servings

PER SERVING:
(1/6 recipe)
Calories 190
Protein 9 g
Carbohydrates 24 g
Fiber 5 g
Fat 6 g
Saturated Fat 3 g
Cholesterol 9 mg
Sodium 336 mg

Grilled Veggie Bites with Spicy Salsa

There is no such thing as too many vegetables in a diet. Grilling the veggies makes them more exciting than the typical raw ones, and they become a wonderful dipper in salsa. Grilled veggies sprinkled with caribe chile are a feisty enough treat even without a dip. These are particularly wonderful served to guests while grilling the rest of the meal, as they can be the first items on the grill and enjoyed while everything else is cooking.

2 5- to 6-inch-long zucchini, rinsed and sliced lengthwise into ¼-inch-thick slices

1 large or 2 small red onions, sliced crosswise into 1-inch-thick slices

1 tablespoon caribe red chile flakes, crushed

1 cup any spicy salsa, such as Hot New Mexican Table Salsa (page 168)

Place the vegetables on a baking sheet. Sprinkle the chile flakes on both sides. Meanwhile, heat the grill to medium high, placing the rack about 3 inches from the coals or flame.

When the fire is hot, grill the onions for about 10 minutes, or until soft. Turn, and add the zucchini; grill for about 2 minutes, then turn again and grill on the other side. The vegetables should be almost fork-tender and browned in places. Cut the zucchini into 1-inch-wide strips. Serve the zucchini and onions with a bowl of toothpicks and a bowl of the salsa.

Cooking Time: 14 minutes, Yield: 4 servings

PER SERVING:
Calories 55
Protein 3 g
Carbohydrates 12 g
Fiber 4 g
Fat 1 g
Saturated Fat 0 g
Cholesterol 0 mg
Sodium 75 mg

Quickie Quesos

These are really naked nachos in a way. They do not have refried beans, which have become quite predictable on nachos. For a light meal, I like to have these with salsa and perhaps some grilled meat or chicken if available. ♪

6 corn tortillas, any kind

1 cup Cheddar and Monterey Jack cheeses, coarsely grated and mixed

¼ cup caribe chile, coarsely grated

3 green chiles, peeled and chopped, or 1 4-ounce can chopped green chiles

Preheat the oven to 425 degrees F. Arrange the tortillas on a baking sheet. Place in the oven and bake for 6 to 8 minutes, until slightly crisp. Remove from the oven and sprinkle evenly with the cheese.

Return to the oven and bake for 2 to 3 minutes more, until the cheese is melted. Remove from the oven and sprinkle with the caribe and green chiles. Cut each tortilla on a cutting board into 4 pieces and arrange as desired on a warm platter. (Warm the platter while the cheese is melting.) Serve warm.

Variations: Olives, chilied meat, or most any pizza topping can be used to top these tortillas. Salsas are great for dunking.

Cooking Time: 8 to 10 minutes, Yield: 6 servings

PER SERVING:
Calories 154
Protein 7 g
Carbohydrates 17 g
Fiber 3 g
Fat 8 g
Saturated Fat 4 g
Cholesterol 18 mg
Sodium 203 mg

Quesadillas

Quesadillas are one of the most versatile of all light meals or appetizers. Restaurants in Old Mexico serve a much simpler version of quesadillas. There, generally a quesadilla is a freshly baked corn tortilla oozing with quick-melting cheese and served with a side dish of freshly made salsa. Sometimes they are fried, though often not. Quesadillas are one of the most fun foods to garnish and present in creative and pretty ways. Innovation is the key to a great quesadilla; just use your favorite or on-hand ingredients and let your imagination roll. 🌶

1 teaspoon unsalted butter, melted

1 wheat-flour tortilla (10- to 12-inch size)

2 to 4 tablespoons grated Monterey Jack and Cheddar cheese combination or any substitution, such as goat cheese, asadero, or other quick-melting cheese

6 to 8 slices pickled jalapeños

Other fillings as desired: sautéed chorizo, sliced grilled chicken, baby shrimp, cooked pinto or black beans, chilied meats, any sliced seared vegetables, chopped onion and tomato

Preheat a comal (Mexican flat griddle), tapa, or griddle to medium heat. Brush some of the butter lightly in the shape of half a tortilla on one side of the comal.

Place the tortilla on the butter. Place the cheese on the buttered half of the tortilla, allowing a ½-inch margin around the edge of the tortilla. Scatter the jalapeño slices and any other fillings over the cheese.

When the cheese starts to melt, fold the other half of the tortilla over the fillings and lightly press until the edges hold together. Brush the top with more of the butter. Flip the quesadilla by gently placing a pancake turner under the curved edges of the quesadilla and rolling it over. Cook until browned. Remove from the heat, slice into 4 or more sections, and garnish as desired. Serve warm.

Cooking Time: 2 to 3 minutes, Yield: 1 quesadilla

PER SERVING:
Calories 326
Protein 10 g
Carbohydrates 41 g
Fiber 2 g
Fat 13 g
Saturated Fat 6 g
Cholesterol 24 mg
Sodium 510 mg

Stuffed Jalapeños

These are quick to make and surprisingly good, if you like it hot! The peanut butter or goat cheese make the jalapeño milder than does the shrimp. Squirting lime juice on the shrimp will make it milder. A good friend of mine, Sam Arnold, serves these in his Fort Restaurant in Denver.

18 whole pickled jalapeños
¼ cup peanut butter, preferably crunchy
¼ cup spicy southwestern-flavored goat cheese (see page 39)
6 large shrimp, cooked, peeled, and deveined

Slit each jalapeño lengthwise. Remove the seeds and blot out excess juice.

Stuff 6 jalapeños with the peanut butter, 6 with the cheese, and 6 with the shrimp. Serve on an attractive platter as finger food.

Preparation Time: 15 minutes, Yield: 6 servings

PER SERVING:
(1 jalapeño)
Calories 67
Protein 3 g
Carbohydrates 3 g
Fiber 1 g
Fat 5 g
Saturated Fat 1 g
Cholesterol 0 mg
Sodium 112 mg
(Analyzed with
Peanut Butter.)

PER SERVING:
(1 jalapeño)
Calories 31
Protein 2 g
Carbohydrates 1 g
Fiber 0 g
Fat 2 g
Saturated Fat 2 g
Cholesterol 5 mg
Sodium 98 mg
(Analyzed with
goat cheese.)

PER SERVING:
(1 jalapeño)
Calories 9
Protein 1 g
Carbohydrates 1 g
Fiber 0 g
Fat 0 g
Saturated Fat 0 g
Cholesterol 11 mg
Sodium 73 mg
(Analyzed with shrimp.)

Double Corned Fritters with Quick-Smoked Shrimp and Jalapeño Lime Cream Dressing

This recipe is not as quick as most of the others; however, for a little more impressive appetizer, they are great and do make a light meal when eaten along with a salad. For entertaining, the batter and dressing can be made ahead and the shrimp can be smoked days beforehand. 🦐

2 ears yellow corn, grilled (can be leftover)
1 large egg
1 ¼ cups buttermilk
1 tablespoon vegetable oil
¼ cup green chile, chopped
½ cup yellow or blue cornmeal or corn flour
½ cup all-purpose flour
½ teaspoon baking soda
1 teaspoon baking powder
¾ teaspoon salt
16 Quick-Smoked Shrimp (recipe follows)
Jalapeño Lime Cream Dressing (page 167)

Cut the corn off the cob; set aside. Combine the egg, buttermilk, oil, and chile and mix well. Combine the cornmeal, flour, baking soda, baking powder, and salt. Add to the buttermilk mixture. Stir just until blended, them stir in the corn. Preheat a griddle. Ladle enough batter onto the griddle to make 12 to 18 2-inch pancakes. Arrange 3 per serving in a somewhat vertical, overlapping stack with the shrimp. Serve with the Jalapeño Lime Cream Dressing or a salsa of your choice and sour cream.

To Quick Smoke Shrimp: Preheat oven to 425 degrees F. Rinse the shrimp and season with salt and pepper and squeeze of lime. Set aside. In the bottom of a heavy pot with a close-fitting cover that will not be damaged by smoke, place black tea leaves or contents of 1 tea bag. Place a metal trivet in the bottom of the pot. Place on high heat of burner and cook until smoke develops, about 3 to 5 minutes. Remove lid and arrange shrimp on trivet. Place the lid on the pot, then move the pot to the oven for 5 minutes.

Cooking Time: 1 minute each, Yield: 4 to 6 servings (12 to 18 fritters)

PER SERVING:
(1/6 recipe)
Calories 216
Protein 12 g
Carbohydrates 31 g
Fiber 2 g
Fat 5 g
Saturated Fat 1 g
Cholesterol 65 mg
Sodium 610 mg

Main Dish Salads

Southwestern-themed main dish salads are quite
popular for lunch or a light dinner. These are all
innovative—not a taco salad in sight. I have paired
grilled or chilied meats with a range of greens, rice,
and other ingredients. To cut the calories, I have
created easy-to-make dressings. They add a fresh,
spicy accent.

Grilled Chicken and Chard Salad

Grilled chicken breast is the darling of fast, low-fat meals. It is quick and easy to prepare and really stunning with the chard, which you can prepare easily on a stovetop grill.

2 boneless, skinless chicken breast halves (6 ounces each)
1 teaspoon Basic Rub (page 176)
1 bunch of red Swiss chard (12 to 16 ounces)
1 large Spanish-style white onion
¼ cup Cilantro Salsa (page 173) or Tomatillo Salsa (page 170)

Trim the chicken, removing all fat and membrane. Rinse, pat dry, and evenly sprinkle with rub and rub into surfaces of chicken. Rinse the chard and cut into 2-inch-wide strips. Slice the onion in half lengthwise, then cut it crosswise into ½-inch-wide strips.

Preheat a large, heavy, well-seasoned skillet until hot. If necessary, spray the skillet with nonstick oil. Grill the onion for about 3 minutes; stir until the edges blacken somewhat. Stir and push the onions to the side and add the chicken breast. Cook for 4 minutes, then turn the chicken and cook for another 4 minutes.

When the onion is somewhat soft and the edges are browned, remove from the skillet. Place the chard in the skillet off to one side. Check for chicken doneness by pressing with your finger. The chicken should be firm to the touch and, when sliced, white inside. Remove the chicken to a cutting board.

Cover the skillet and sear the chard until some of the leaves are blackened and wilted on the edges. To serve, arrange the chard in a strip down the center of each plate. Arrange the onion in a row on each side of the chard. Cut the chicken into ½-inch-wide slices and center it in a row on the chard. Top with the salsa.

Cooking Time: 10 to 12 minutes, Yield: 2 large or 4 small servings

PER SERVING:
(1/4 recipe)
Calories 138
Protein 20 g
Carbohydrates 10 g
Fiber 3 g
Fat 2 g
Saturated Fat 1 g
Cholesterol 47 mg
Sodium 308 mg
(Analyzed with Cilantro Salsa.)

Chicken Rice Salad with Jalapeño Lime Cream Dressing

Here green chiles supply the capsaicin or spiciness. Green chiles are merely unripe red chiles and possess the same measure of capsaicin as though they were red, ripe chiles. This quick to make main dish salad, complements of convenience or deli ingredients, is a quick and healthy, spicy entrée for lunch or dinner. ♪

1 6-ounce package southwestern-flavored rice mix
¾ pound boneless, skinless deli chicken, diced
1 4-ounce can diced green chiles
¼ cup Jalapeño Lime Cream Dressing (page 167)
Optional garnishes: ¼ cup ripe olives, sliced; 1 head of red or green leaf lettuce, rinsed and torn into bite-size pieces

Cook the rice according to package directions. Set aside to cool.
Place the chicken, chiles, pepper, and rice in a large bowl and toss with the salad dressing. Add the olives, if desired. To serve, divide the salad among 4 plates, on top of the lettuce, if using.
Cooking Time: 10 to 12 minutes, Yield: 4 servings

PER SERVING:
Calories 333
Protein 32 g
Carbohydrates 38 g
Fiber 4 g
Fat 7 g
Saturated Fat 3 g
Cholesterol 80 mg
Sodium 767 mg
(Analyzed with 1 tablespoon butter called for in the package of rice mix.)

Terrific Scallop Tostado Salad

This main dish salad is very easy on the waistline, weighing in at fewer than 200 calories. It is very flavorful, possessing the health-spice "hit" from red chile in the rub and green jalapeño in the dressing—both adequate for supplying enough capsaicin to assist your body in becoming a healthier you!

1 pound bay scallops

2 teaspoons Basic Rub (page 176) or favorite commercial rub

6 cups salad greens, rinsed, torn, and drained

4 tablespoons Jalapeño Lime Cream Dressing or Spicy Cilantro Lime Dressing (page 167)

16 baked corn tortilla tostado triangles or toasts (page 36)

Rinse the scallops and pat dry with a paper towel. Place the scallops on a paper plate, sprinkle with the rub, and toss to coat. Set aside.

Preheat a heavy, seasoned, nonstick skillet over medium-high heat; spray the skillet with nonstick spray if necessary.

Quickly sear the scallops, stirring a few times to cook evenly, for 1 ½ to 2 minutes, just until done. They will seize up as they cook yet should still be moist and tender.

To serve, divide the salad greens evenly among the plates, top each with the scallops, and drizzle each with 1 tablespoon of the dressing. Stab tostado triangles into the top, bottom, and each side of the salad at the 6, 9, 12, and 3 o'clock positions. Serve warm.

Cooking time: 4 minutes, Yield: 4 servings

PER SERVING:
Calories 145
Protein 13 g
Carbohydrates 18 g
Fiber 3 g
Fat 3 g
Saturated Fat 0 g
Cholesterol 18 mg
Sodium 640 mg

Spinach, Shrimp, and Pear Salad with Piñons

The fresh, mellow flavor of pear is a wonderful alternative to the predictable mushrooms in a spinach salad! Shrimp and piñons add a flavor balance that is greatly complemented by the gusto of the Hotter-Than-Fire Dressing.

1 12-ounce package fresh spinach

2 ripe Bartlett or d'Anjou pears

¾ pound small, cooked shrimp, peeled and deveined

¼ cup Hotter-Than-Fire Dressing (page 166)

Freshly ground black pepper

2 tablespoons roasted piñons

Place the spinach first in a colander and spray water over it, then place it in a salad spinner to drain.

Slice the pears in half lengthwise; remove the core (but leave the peel), then cut the fruit into thin wedges.

Place the spinach and shrimp in a salad bowl and toss with the dressing. Add ground pepper, if desired.

To serve, divide the spinach mixture among the plates or bowls and top with the pear wedges (place pear wedges all in the same direction). Sprinkle with piñons and serve.

Preparation Time: 6 to 8 minutes, Yield: 2 large or 4 small servings

PER SERVING:
(1/4 recipe)
Calories 197
Protein 21 g
Carbohydrates 17 g
Fiber 5 g
Fat 6 g
Saturated Fat 1 g
Cholesterol 166 mg
Sodium 302 mg

Spicy Beef and Potato Salad with Hot Red Chile Dressing

The chiles in the rub really accentuate the hearty, beefy flavor that is so complemented by the butter-infused baby red potatoes and caramelized onions. This salad pleases all—the weight conscious salad eaters and the "meat and potatoes" set. The Hot Red Chile Dressing is just the right flavor finish.

¾ pound beef sirloin tip, well trimmed

1 teaspoon Basic Rub (page 176)

1 ½ pounds baby red potatoes, well scrubbed

2 teaspoons unsalted butter

2 cups mixed baby greens (available in the produce section of the supermarket)

1 large onion, halved and thinly sliced into rings

¼ cup Hot Red Chile Dressing (page 166)

Using a tenderizer mallet, pound the beef to about ¼-inch thick. Add the rub to both sides of the beef; set aside. Place the potatoes in boiling salted water, cover, and cook for 12 to 15 minutes, until fork-tender. Drain the potatoes and add 1 teaspoon of the butter; stir and cover. Meanwhile, place the greens in a salad spinner; rinse, spin, and set aside.

While the potatoes are cooking, in a well-seasoned or nonstick skillet over medium heat, place the remaining teaspoon of the butter and coat the bottom of the pan. Add the onion; cover and cook for about 3 minutes, stirring occasionally, until the onions start to sweat and become limp. Uncover and cook for about another 2 minutes, or until golden, stirring occasionally. Remove onions from pan.

Increase the heat to high and add the beef. Sauté for about 1 ½ minutes per side for medium-rare beef, which is the juiciest. Remove to a cutting board.

Cut the beef into ¼-inch-thick slices, then cut each slice into 2-inch lengths. Place in a salad bowl. Add the potatoes, onion, greens, and dressing; toss together. Serve immediately.

Cooking Time: 20 minutes, Yield: 4 servings

PER SERVING:
(1/4 recipe)
Calories 314
Protein 23 g
Carbohydrates 36 g
Fiber 4 g
Fat 9 g
Saturated Fat 4 g
Cholesterol 58 mg
Sodium 229 mg

Carne Adobado Stir Fried Slaw

Strange sounding name: Carne adobado is actually a favorite, traditional northern New Mexican pork dish that was conquistador-inspired. Pork and chiles were meant for each other. Because this salad combines spice, crunch, and color, you may want to serve it solo or precede it with a cup of creamy soup, such as Chicken Tortilla Chowder (page 130) or Chile-Sparked Sweet Potato Soup (page 124).

1 pork tenderloin (about 1 ¼ pounds)

¼ cup crushed red caribe chile (or ground pure mild red chile for a milder flavor)

1 large clove garlic

1 teaspoon each Mexican oregano and freshly ground cumin

3 cups shredded coleslaw base, preferably red cabbage (available in the produce section of the supermarket) or hand-shredded red cabbage

⅓ cup cider vinegar

Trim the tenderloin of any fat and sinew-like casing. Cut the meat into slices about ¼-inch thick.

In a blender, place ¾ cup water and add the chile, garlic, oregano, and cumin. Process until thick. Pour the mixture into a 1-quart microwavable baking pan (see Note). Add the pork slices and stir to mix. Cover with wax paper and cook in the microwave oven for 5 minutes. Stir, check the pork for doneness, and cook for 2 more minutes if needed, or until the pink color disappears. Add the cabbage and vinegar and stir to mix. Taste for flavor balance, adjusting if necessary. Cover again with the wax paper and cook for 2 minutes. To serve, arrange the cabbage on the plates and top with the pork strips.

Note: For stovetop cooking, place the pork and the sauce in a deep skillet or a 5-quart Dutch oven. Bring to a simmer and cook for 10 minutes, or until the pork is no longer pink. Add the cabbage and vinegar, cover, and cook for 3 to 4 minutes, until the cabbage is slightly wilted.

Cooking Time: 5 to 7 minutes in a microwave oven, 13 to 14 minutes in a conventional oven, Yield: 4 servings

PER SERVING:
Calories 210
Protein 31 g
Carbohydrates 7 g
Fiber 3 g
Fat 6 g
Saturated Fat 2 g
Cholesterol 84 mg
Sodium 73 mg

Beef, Pork, & Lamb

When thinking of southwestern foods, many
of us think of beef—as it has long been a main-
stay. The ranches of the West developed huge herds
more than a century ago and have continuously been
a major source of meat. Many of the traditional chile
stews and dishes require long slow simmering, hence
are not given to quick preparation and therefore
are not included in this chapter. Several of the
other books I have written feature those recipes.
Both the quick and not-so-quick recipes lend
themselves to batch cooking and freezing. The
recipes that follow are quick, fun, spicy, and full
of chiles…great for lean eating.

Chile Rubbed, Grilled Rib Eye Steak

Lemon and garlic complement the chile in the rub for this yummy steak. If
desired, serve topped with sautéed mushrooms mentioned in the variation
along with green chile. You can have these steaks ready in 15 minutes—
start to finish—if you preheat the grill first.

1 ½ to 2 pounds rib eye steaks, 1 inch thick
½ medium lemon
2 teaspoons ground pure hot red chile
2 cloves garlic, minced (or 1 teaspoon garlic granules or powdered garlic)
Ground black pepper

Trim any excess fat off the edge of the meat. To prevent curling, cut every
2 inches about ¼ inch deep into the flesh. Prepare the outdoor grill, or
preheat the broiler or stovetop grill to high.

Squeeze the lemon on both sides of each steak. Combine the chile
and garlic and rub half of the mixture on each side. Add several
grinds of pepper to each.

Cook for 7 minutes on one side and 6 minutes on the other.
Serve at once.

Variation: While grilling the steak, sauté 6 to 8 mushrooms in a
tablespoon of butter until soft; top the steak before serving. For a
delicious garnish, add warm parched green chile (fresh, frozen, or
canned) to top of the steak.

Cooking Time: 13 minutes for medium rare, Yield: 3 or 4 servings

PER SERVING:
(¼ recipe)
Calories 290
Protein 35 g
Carbohydrates 1 g
Fiber 0 g
Fat 15 g
Saturated Fat 7 g
Cholesterol 101 mg
Sodium 88 mg

Beef Enchilada Bake

This hearty favorite is a wonderful make-ahead dish. You can prepare several and have them on hand in the freezer. In New Mexico, enchiladas are generally served flat, as suggested here. 🌶

1 pound ground chuck (80 percent lean)
2 cups Basic Red Chile Sauce (page 164)
8 corn tortillas, any kind
½ cup onion, chopped
1 cup Cheddar and Monterey Jack cheeses, grated and mixed
Lettuce and tomato, chopped for garnish

Sauté the beef in a heavy skillet over medium heat, breaking up all lumps and cook for about 5 minutes, or until the pink color is almost gone. Drain off any visible fat. Add the chile sauce to the beef.

Preheat the oven to 375 degrees F. Using an 8 x 10- or 9 x 9-inch baking dish or pan, pour in some of the meat sauce, then a layer of 4 tortillas, then more sauce, half the onion, and half the grated cheeses. Add the remaining 4 tortillas, sauce, onion, and cheeses. Bake for 12 to 15 minutes, until the cheese bubbles and the mixture cooks together. Serve garnished with the lettuce and chopped tomato.

Cooking Time: 17 to 20 minutes, Yield: 4 servings

PER SERVING:
Calories 531
Protein 32 g
Carbohydrates 38 g
Fiber 7 g
Fat 29 g
Saturated Fat 14 g
Cholesterol 108 mg
Sodium 677 mg

PER SERVING:
Calories 469
Protein 37 g
Carbohydrates 38 g
Fiber 7 g
Fat 19 g
Saturated Fat 8 g
Cholesterol 63 mg
Sodium 727 mg
(Analyzed using 91 percent lean beef and low-fat cheese.)

Salsa Beef Stir Fry

You can fire this one up to your heart's content with as hot a salsa as you can enjoy. Additional chile can be added. This is a hearty all-in-one dish that is quick to make and can be varied to suit your taste and to what ingredients are on hand.

1 pound extra-lean ground beef (92 percent lean, see Note)
1 cup tomato-based salsa
1 15 ¼-ounce can whole kernel corn, drained, or 1 10-ounce package frozen
8 ounces dry, uncooked pasta, blue corn, green chile, or plain fussili (see Note)
Cheddar and Monterey Jack cheeses, grated (for accompaniment, optional)

Sauté the beef in a heavy, nonstick skillet, making sure no lumps remain. Drain off any visible fat. To the beef add the remaining ingredients. Stir well, to coat the pasta. Cover and simmer for 6 to 8 minutes or until done. Taste and adjust the seasonings.

Serve with a side dish of the grated cheeses, if desired.

Note: Round steak cut into thin strips, such as for Asian dishes, is a good substitute for the ground beef, if preferred. You can use most any kind of pasta—even spaghetti or capellini broken into 3- to 4-inch lengths. Using leftover cooked pasta will shorten the cooking time.

Cooking Time: 13 to 15 minutes, Yield: 4 servings

PER SERVING:
Calories 455
Protein 33 g
Carbohydrates 56 g
Fiber 5 g
Fat 12 g
Saturated Fat 4 g
Cholesterol 41 mg
Sodium 255 mg

Seared Chile Pork Tossed with Pasta

Somewhat reminiscent of stroganoff with the creamy texture supplied by nonfat sour cream, this dish only needs a simple salad to complete a main meal. Additional veggies can be added if desired. With the creaminess, some hot minced jalapeño, or whatever chile you prefer, could be stirred into it. 🎵

12 ounces pork tenderloin

1 tablespoon Basic Rub (page 176)

10 ounces fusilli, cooked (can be a flavored pasta, such as cilantro, jalapeño, or blue corn)

1 tablespoon unsalted butter

3 cloves garlic, minced

¼ cup nonfat sour cream

½ cup tomato-based salsa

Trim the pork of all fat and sinew and cut it into ¾-inch squares. To coat the pieces of pork, shake them with the rub in a plastic bag, or toss them in a bowl.

Heat a well-seasoned, heavy skillet. Add butter and garlic. When garlic becomes clear, add the pork cubes. Cook quickly on medium-high heat to brown all sides. Cook pork until crisp on the outside and juicy inside.

Stir in the sour cream and salsa. When well blended, add the pasta and toss together and serve.

Cooking time: 8 to 10 minutes, Yield: 4 servings

PER SERVING:
Calories 262
Protein 23 g
Carbohydrates 26 g
Fiber 2 g
Fat 7 g
Saturated Fat 3 g
Cholesterol 59 mg
Sodium 662 mg

Aztec Style Pork Chops

You've got to give the Aztecs credit for chipotles—they are the spicy, subtly smoky red jalapeños that give this recipe a super punch. The honey and cinnamon pair beautifully with the pork and serve to make for a lacquered brown on the outside of the chops. You are set here with spice for a very healthy entrée. I like these served with spiced steamed spinach and whipped sweet potatoes—special enough for company. 🌶

2 dried chipotle chiles, reconstituted (see instructions below), minced

4 cloves garlic, minced

¼ cup honey

1 ½ teaspoons ground cinnamon

1 tablespoon ground pure mild red chile

4 pork loin chops (1-inch thick), trimmed of excess fat

4 cinnamon sticks

4 slices jicama, each ¼-inch thick

In a shallow bowl, combine the drained chiles, garlic, honey, ground cinnamon, and ground chile. Add enough chipotle cooking liquid to make a thick paste. Marinate for 10 to 15 minutes. Preheat the grill, stovetop grill, or a large, heavy, seasoned skillet to medium high. Grill the chops for 8 minutes per side. At the same time and on the same surface, grill the jicama until it is slightly edged with brown on each side. To serve, top each chop with a cinnamon stick. Overlap each chop with a slice of the grilled jicama.

Reconstituted chipotles: To reconstitute chipotles in a microwave oven, place the pods in a 4-cup glass measuring cup. Cover with water and add 1 teaspoon cider vinegar. Cover with plastic wrap and cook for 5 minutes, on full power or until the skin slips on the flesh.

Cooking Time: 16 minutes, Yield: 4 servings

PER SERVING:
Calories 281
Protein 25 g
Carbohydrates 20 g
Fiber 1 g
Fat 11 g
Saturated Fat 4 g
Cholesterol 70 mg
Sodium 53 mg

Chile Sage Pork Chops

The flavor of the pork chops is best if fresh sage can be used. Other aromatic herbs such as rosemary can be substituted. The Black Eyed Pea Salsa and Chipotle and Roasted Garlic Mashed Potatoes can be as fiery as you like!

8 cloves garlic, minced

1 tablespoon extra-virgin olive oil, preferably Spanish

¼ cup fresh sage leaves, minced

2 tablespoons ground pure hot red New Mexican chile

4 large pork chops, ½- to 1-inch thick, trimmed, rinsed, and patted dry

Black-eyed Pea Salsa (page 175), optional

Chipotle and Roasted Garlic Mashed Potatoes (page 148), optional

If grilling, prepare the grill. Using a mini-chopper, purée the garlic. Add the oil and sage and grind finely. Place the mixture in a small bowl and stir in the chile.

Evenly coat both sides of the chops with the mixture and rub it in. Grill or broil the chops, or pan-sear them in a hot, heavy skillet. Cook for 5 to 8 minutes per side for medium-well, until the meat is light pink and registers 165 degrees F. on a meat thermometer.

Cooking Time: 10 to 16 minutes, Yield: 4 servings

PER SERVING:
Calories 264
Protein 26 g
Carbohydrates 5 g
Fiber 2 g
Fat 15 g
Saturated Fat 5 g
Cholesterol 70 mg
Sodium 53 mg

Grilled Veal Chops with Just Peachy Salsa

The tender, delicate flavor of veal is complemented by fruit with a "kick." If you are grilling the veal outdoors, grill vegetables to go along with it, such as sweet potatoes with honey butter and zucchini or asparagus with lime and chile. ♪

4 veal chops (¾-inch thick), trimmed of excess fat

1 tablespoon extra-virgin olive oil, preferably Spanish

2 cloves garlic, minced

Several grinds of pepper (green peppercorns, if available)

1 cup Just Peachy Salsa (page 175)

Rinse the veal, pat dry, and set aside. Combine the oil, garlic, and ground pepper. Rub seasoning mixture evenly on both sides of each chop.

Preheat the grill, stovetop grill, or a heavy, seasoned skillet until hot. Grill the chops for 4 to 5 minutes per side. Serve napped with the salsa.

Cooking time: 10 minutes, Yield: 4 servings

PER SERVING:
Calories 250
Protein 30 g
Carbohydrates 15 g
Fiber 4 g
Fat 8 g
Saturated Fat 2 g
Cholesterol 91 mg
Sodium 74 mg

Lamb Fajitas

Lamb is meant for garlic! Here the fresh lime juice and pequin chile are perfect accents, especially when paired with a Pico de Gallo made with honeydew melon substituted for the tomato and fresh mint instead of cilantro. I am a huge fan of lamb, and it is outstanding here, as well as very healthy, low in calories, and without fat.

Juice of 1 lime (about 1 ½ tablespoons juice)
4 cloves garlic, minced
1 tablespoon extra-virgin olive oil, preferably Spanish
Several grinds of black pepper
1 ½ pounds leg of lamb or sirloin, sliced ¼-inch thick, fat trimmed and removed
8 white-flour tortillas, warmed
Pico de Gallo (page 174), for garnish

In a shallow, nonreactive bowl, combine the lime juice, garlic, oil, and ground pepper. Tenderize the lamb with a meat tenderizer.

Place the lamb slices, one at a time, in the lime mixture, pressing the mixture into one side of each slice, then turning the slice and pressing the mixture into the other side.

Preheat the grill, stovetop grill, or a heavy, nonstick skillet until hot. Sear the meat for 2 to 3 minutes per side. Remove and slice into ¾-inch strips. Serve in the tortillas with Pico de Gallo.

Cooking Time: 4 to 6 minutes, Yield: 4 servings

PER SERVING:
Calories 784
Protein 46 g
Carbohydrates 95 g
Fiber 6 g
Fat 24 g
Saturated Fat 7 g
Cholesterol 100 mg
Sodium 795 mg
(Analyzed with two 10-inch flour tortillas, Pico de Gallo, and nonfat sour cream.)

Lamb Chops with Jalapeño Jelly

To me, lamb is so much more wonderful when accompanied by hot, jalapeño jelly—homemade if at all possible—than it is with mint jelly. White bean salsa, spiked with fresh jalapeño, gives a double whammy of spice and is truly finger lickin' good. (I bet everyone at your table will be picking up the lamb bones to get the last remaining morsels of succulent lamb.)

8 loin or rib lamb chops (1-inch thick), trimmed of excess fat

3 cloves garlic, minced

1 tablespoon Mexican oregano, chopped, or 1 teaspoon dried

1 ½ tablespoons extra-virgin olive oil, preferably Spanish

3 tablespoons jalapeño jelly

White Bean Salsa (page 173)

Rinse the lamb chops and pat dry. In a mini-chopper or blender, place the garlic, oregano, and oil and process until smooth. Smear the mixture onto both sides of each chop as uniformly as possible.

Preheat the grill, stovetop grill, or a heavy, seasoned, nonstick skillet until hot. Grill or sear the chops for 4 to 5 minutes per side. Serve on a bed of the white beans with the two chop bones vertically intertwined. Place ¼ of the jalapeño jelly atop each pair of lamb chops.

Cooking Time: 8 to 10 minutes, Yield: 4 servings

PER SERVING:
Calories 362
Protein 38 g
Carbohydrates 12 g
Fiber 1 g
Fat 17 g
Saturated Fat 6 g
Cholesterol 119 mg
Sodium 112 mg

Chicken & Turkey

Chicken takes well to the bright, clear flavors of chiles, cilantro, and southwestern spices. Chicken breast in particular is the darling of low-fat, quick cooking. As a cost savings, whenever you see chicken breasts on sale, buy extra. To freeze them, just trim excess fat, if any, then rinse, pat dry, and place on a wax paper-lined baking sheet. When they are frozen solid, place in a plastic bag, label, and seal. To thaw, place them on a plate, cover with plastic wrap, and place in the refrigerator. Quick thawing is best done in a sealed plastic bag in warm water.

I have included some traditional favorites, such as the chilaquiles, a must try, Soft Chicken Tacos, and yummy Sweetheart Barbecued Chicken, which is flavored with chile, honey, and balsamic vinegar and is easy to prepare.

The subtle flavor of turkey seems to require a few more than five ingredients, but the dishes are still quick to prepare. My husband, Gordon, particularly likes Turkey Chili with a Margarita Splash.

Chicken with Rice Skillet

Chicken and rice dishes abound in Mediterranean and Mexican cuisines. I tailored this recipe to have the creamy chicken broth-based sauce rather than the tomatoey one, as this is my flavor preference. Coupled with a simple tossed salad, you will have a delicious meal. 🌶

2 cups uncooked quick-cooking long-grain rice

2 whole boneless, skinless chicken breasts or 6 to 8 boneless, skinless thighs

1 to 2 4-ounce cans chopped green chiles

1 14 ½-ounce can chicken broth

1 5-ounce can evaporated milk or ⅔ cup evaporated skim milk

Place the rice in a heavy, deep, seasoned skillet, then add the chicken, chiles, broth, and milk.

Cook, covered, over high heat until the sauce simmers, then reduce the heat to low and cook for 15 minutes. Uncover and check for doneness. Taste and adjust the flavoring. Serve hot.

Variation: For added color and flavor, add a 4-ounce jar of pimiento strips.

Cooking Time: 19 to 20 minutes, Yield: 4 servings

PER SERVING:
Calories 542
Protein 39 g
Carbohydrates 84 g
Fiber 3 g
Fat 4 g
Saturated Fat 1 g
Cholesterol 77 mg
Sodium 825 mg
(Analyzed with chicken breast, low-sodium broth, and evaporated skim milk.)

Quick Cilantro Chicken

Cilantro is a spice tamer; however, it is also delicate. The tender leaves wilt quite quickly, and if chopped too finely, the flavor becomes strong and disagreeable. So always remember to coarsely chop and add the cilantro just before cooking or serving. The chile in this dish can be varied. If no pequin is available, add the chile or hot sauce of your choice.

1 ½ pounds boneless, skinless chicken breast tenders or 4 chicken breast halves

8 cloves garlic, minced

2 tablespoons extra-virgin olive oil, preferably Spanish

1 ½ teaspoons Dijon mustard

¼ cup cilantro, coarsely chopped

1 teaspoon crushed pequin quebrado

4 lime wedges, for garnish (optional)

Rinse the chicken breasts and pat dry. Combine the garlic, oil, mustard, cilantro, and pequin. Generously coat the chicken pieces.

Preheat the grill, stovetop grill, or a heavy, seasoned skillet. Add the chicken and cook for 3 to 4 minutes per side, turning only once, when the chicken starts to curl at the edges and feels firm to the touch. Serve garnished with a lime wedge, if desired.

Cooking Time: 6 to 8 minutes, Yield: 4 servings

PER SERVING:
Calories 253
Protein 35 g
Carbohydrates 2 g
Fiber 0 g
Fat 11 g
Saturated Fat 2 g
Cholesterol 94 mg
Sodium 108 mg

Chicken Chilaquiles con Salsa

Chilaquiles quickly become a favorite with most anyone who tries them. They are not as common in the United States as in Mexico, having originated in Central and Southern Mexico, particularly the Yucatan. The Mayans have such a knack with them, and this recipe is from the very successful Melia Mayan hotel in Cozumel where we conducted a class on the Spanish influences on southwestern cuisine. Chiles in the salsa increase the healthful aspects of the dish. More chiles, red or green, can be added for increased zip and health!

Nonstick oil spray

8 corn tortillas

1 pound chicken breasts, approximately

1 cup tomato-based salsa

1 ½ cups chicken broth

¼ cup crumbled asadero, feta, or grated Jack cheese

¼ cup low- or nonfat sour cream, plus 4 teaspoons for garnish (optional)

Preheat the oven to 350 degrees F. Spray a 2-quart baking dish (8x8-inch, 9-inch round, or 10-inch oblong) with nonstick oil spray. Cut the tortillas into sixths and place in the dish in an even layer.

Cook the chicken breasts covered in ½ cup of the broth in a saucepan on the stove for 6 to 8 minutes. Allow the chicken to cool. Shred the chicken and arrange over the tortillas. Top with the salsa, broth, and cheese. Add 4 teaspoons of sour cream, if desired, and bake until bubbly and heated through. Serve hot. Garnish each serving with a dollop of sour cream, if desired.

Cooking Time: 15 minutes, Yield: 4 servings

PER SERVING:
Calories 348
Protein 41 g
Carbohydrates 28 g
Fiber 4 g
Fat 8 g
Saturated Fat 3 g
Cholesterol 106 mg
Sodium 408 mg
(Analyzed with commercial salsa, asadero cheese, and no optional ingredients.)

Soft Chicken Tacos

The original taco, a child's snack prepared when the mother was busy cooking a meal, is the best version. They are made with freshly-prepared corn tortillas wrapped around whatever ingredients one wishes. Lacking the time to make tortillas, use purchased tortillas and warm just before serving.

1 pound boneless, skinless chicken breasts
1 tablespoon Basic Rub (page 176)
8 fresh corn tortillas
Romaine lettuce, finely shredded
½ cup Tomatillo Salsa (page 170) or purchased salsa

Rinse the chicken and pat dry. Pound with a tenderizer mallet or the flat side of a heavy knife. Rub each side of the breast with the rub.

Wrap the tortillas in aluminum foil and warm them for 5 to 10 minutes or until warm in a 350 degree F. oven, or just before serving, heat them in a plastic bag for 1 minute in the microwave oven.

Preheat a stovetop grill or a griddle. Cook the chicken for 3 to 4 minutes per side, turning only once. (It will be ready to turn when it starts to curl on the edges and feels firm.) Slice into strips and place on half of each tortilla. Top with lettuce and salsa, roll up, and serve.

Cooking Time: 6 to 8 minutes, Yield: 4 servings

PER SERVING:
Calories 255
Protein 27 g
Carbohydrates 28 g
Fiber 4 g
Fat 4 g
Saturated Fat 1 g
Cholesterol 63 mg
Sodium 570 mg

Sweetheart Barbecued Chicken

The tangy, honey-edged spiciness of these barbecued chicken thighs is wonderful. While the grill is heating, place some sweet potato rounds, cut ½-inch thick, on it. To complete the meal, steam green beans, splashed with orange juice, in the microwave oven.

8 chicken thighs, skinned and deboned, fat removed

1 teaspoon ground pure hot chile, or to taste

4 cloves garlic, minced

2 tablespoons honey

2 tablespoons balsamic vinegar

Fresh spinach, for garnish (optional)

Rinse the chicken and pat dry. Combine the chile, garlic, honey, and vinegar. Spoon or brush the mixture evenly over the chicken. Set aside for at least 10 minutes.

Meanwhile, preheat the grill, stovetop grill, or a heavy, seasoned skillet to medium-high. Add the chicken and cook for 4 to 5 minutes, then turn and grill the other side. The chicken is done when it is firm to the touch when pressed or a meat thermometer registers 185 degrees F.

Serve on a bed of fresh spinach, if desired.

Cooking Time: 8 to 10 minutes, Yield: 4 servings

PER SERVING:
Calories 442
Protein 59 g
Carbohydrates 28 g
Fiber 4 g
Fat 10 g
Saturated Fat 3 g
Cholesterol 154 mg
Sodium 450 mg

Pollo Rellenos with Salsa Fresca

Relleno in Spanish means stuffed. Here, I have stuffed the chicken breasts with cheese and green chile, then coated them with a crispy coating. The traditional Salsa Fresca is wonderful as an accompaniment. &

4 boneless, skinless chicken breast halves, trimmed of any fat or sinew (see Note)
2 tablespoons low-fat Cheddar cheese
2 tablespoons chopped green chile (canned or frozen)
¼ cup skim milk or buttermilk
½ cup cornflake crumbs (see Note)
Salsa Fresca (page 169), optional

Rinse the chicken and pat dry. Pound with a tenderizer mallet or the flat side of a heavy knife. Lay the chicken breasts out flat and divide the cheese and chiles among them.

Roll the chicken and fasten with toothpicks or skewers, tucking in the sides to hold the cheese mixture. Dip in the milk to coat uniformly, then dip into the cornflake crumbs. Place in a microwave-safe baking dish, cover with wax paper, and cook on high for 10 to 12 minutes. Meanwhile, combine the Salsa Fresca, if using. Spoon a ribbon of salsa over each serving.

Note: Boneless, skinless thighs can be substituted, if preferred. Cheese-cracker crumbs can be substituted for the cornflake crumbs, but they contain more fat.

Cooking Time: 10 to 12 minutes in a microwave oven, Yield: 4 servings

PER SERVING:
Calories 250
Protein 29 g
Carbohydrates 13 g
Fiber 1 g
Fat 3 g
Saturated Fat 1 g
Cholesterol 74 mg
Sodium 242 mg

Chicken Breasts Baked in Salsa

Prepared salsa, whether commercial or homemade, is a wonderful ingredient. It adds a spicy accent to an otherwise ho-hum preparation. These spicy breasts are placed on a bed of rice or pasta, or for a lighter touch, lettuce can be used.

4 boneless, skinless chicken breast halves (4 to 6 ounces each), trimmed of any fat or sinew

Few drops of vegetable oil or oil spray

1 cup salsa

1 small onion, sliced into thin rings

Cooked rice or pasta, for accompaniment

Southwestern-flavored goat cheese (page 39) or nonfat sour cream, for garnish (optional)

Rinse the chicken and pat dry. Warm the oil in a heavy, seasoned skillet (see Note). Add the chicken and cook for 3 to 4 minutes, until the chicken is lightly browned. Turn and brown the other side for about 3 minutes.

Reduce the heat to low, pour the salsa over the chicken, and scatter with the onion rings. Cover and allow to steam for 4 to 6 minutes, until the chicken is fork-tender.

Serve on rice or pasta, spooning the sauce over the chicken. Top with the goat cheese, if desired.

Note: To cook the chicken in the microwave oven, place the chicken in a baking dish, cook it for 1 ½ minutes per side, top with the salsa and onion rings, and cover tightly. Cook for 7 to 10 minutes, until tender.

Cooking Time: 16 to 20 minutes, Yield: 4 servings

PER SERVING:
Calories 175
Protein 28 g
Carbohydrates 6 g
Fiber 1 g
Fat 4 g
Saturated Fat 0 g
Cholesterol 73 mg
Sodium 133 mg
(Analyzed with ½ teaspoon oil and Hot New Mexican Table Salsa.)

Turkey Enchiladas

Ground turkey is a quick substitute for poached chicken. I like to make enchiladas New Mexico style—flat instead of rolled. For a complete meal, serve with beans—pintos for tradition's sake—or black beans. For added spice, drain the juice and add a few table-spoons of salsa to taste.

SAUCE

1 pound ground turkey breast

1 ½ cups chicken broth (1 14 ½-ounce can)

1 4-ounce can chopped green chiles or ½ cup fresh or frozen parched, peeled, and chopped green chiles (4 to 6 chiles)

¼ teaspoon freshly ground cumin (optional)

ENCHILADAS

8 corn tortillas

1 small onion, chopped

½ cup grated Cheddar and Monterey Jack cheese combination

Romaine lettuce, rinsed and coarsely chopped, for garnish

1 large tomato, cut into 16 wedges, for garnish

To make the sauce, place the turkey in a cold, heavy skillet. Place over medi-um-low heat and stir regularly to break up the lumps. After cooking a minute or two, increase the heat to medium and cook, stirring, for about 5 minutes, or until the meat turns white. Add the broth and stir until the sauce thickens. Reduce the heat to low to keep the sauce warm.

Preheat the oven to 350 degrees F. Place some of the sauce in the center of 4 ovenproof plates. Top each with a tortilla, then a spoonful of sauce, a sprinkle of onion, and 1 tablespoon of the cheese.

Repeat with another tortilla on each plate, topping each with one quarter of the remaining sauce, one quarter of the onion, and 1 tablespoon of the cheese. Place each plate in the oven for about 5 minutes (or the microwave oven for 1 ½ minutes each), or until the filling bubbles. Encircle each enchilada with lettuce and 4 tomato wedges. Serve hot.

Variation: To the sauce add one or two of the following: 10-ounce package frozen, chopped spinach, 1 15 ¼-ounce can whole kernel corn, or 1 15-ounce can black beans.

Cooking Time: 20 minutes, Yield: 4 servings

PER SERVING:
Calories 341
Protein 39 g
Carbohydrates 31 g
Fiber 4 g
Fat 8 g
Saturated Fat 4 g
Cholesterol 98 mg
Sodium 602 mg

Grilled Turkey Tenders

Tenders are the most succulent part of the turkey breast, and are just terrific grilled and served with the spicy onion rings atop a bed of baby greens or spinach.

1 large red onion, sliced into thin rings

½ cup cider vinegar

1 teaspoon crushed red pequin quebrado chile

1 ¼ to 1 ½ pounds turkey tenders, trimmed of any fat or sinew

2 teaspoons extra-virgin olive oil, preferably Spanish

6 cups mixed salad greens

Slice the onion into thin rings. Preheat a large, heavy, seasoned frying pan over medium-high heat. Place the onions in the dry pan and cook, stirring and turning the rings for a minute or two, until they are light tan on the edges and somewhat softened. Remove to a bowl; add the vinegar and chile and stir to mix. Cover to keep warm.

Meanwhile, rinse the turkey tenders and pat dry. Pound with a tenderizer to about ½ inch thick. Slice in lengths so they will fit easily in the frying pan. Lightly and evenly oil the outside of each tender. Grill them for 4 ½ minutes per side, or until the flesh is no longer pink and the turkey is firm to the touch.

Transfer to a cutting board and slice into ½-inch-wide strips.

Arrange a bed of lettuce on each plate. Top with the turkey strips and warm onions and serve.

Cooking Time: 10 to 12 minutes, Yield: 4 servings

PER SERVING:
Calories 252
Protein 46 g
Carbohydrates 7 g
Fiber 2 g
Fat 4 g
Saturated Fat 1 g
Cholesterol 123 mg
Sodium 100 mg

Turkey Chili with a Margarita Splash

Leftover roast turkey makes a marvelous curtain call in this recipe.
Lacking any, you may use sautéed ground turkey—just cook covered
in a microwave for about 2 minutes or cook on a stovetop slightly
longer until the pink color disappears. This versatile recipe can be
varied—any kind of bean can be substituted and red chile can be
substituted for the green.

1 medium onion, chopped

1 14 ½-ounce can low-sodium, low-fat chicken broth

1 4-ounce can chopped green chiles

1 15 ¼-ounce can black beans

2 cups chopped, cooked turkey or 1 pound ground skinless
turkey breast or chicken, sautéed (see Note)

1 ½ teaspoons ground cumin

Optional garnishes: 1 lime, jigger of tequila

Place the onions in a cold, heavy saucepan. Sauté over medium-
high heat for about 2 minutes, or until the onion starts to brown on
the edges. Reduce the heat to medium-low and cook, stirring, for
about 5 minutes, or until the onion darkens or caramelizes in its
own juices. Immediately add the broth, chiles, beans, cooked turkey,
and cumin. Simmer for 8 to 10 minutes.

Serve with about a teaspoon or so each of freshly squeezed lime juice
and tequila.

Note: To sauté the ground turkey in the microwave oven, break up the
lumps, place in a microwavable bowl, and cover. Cook on high for 2 to 3
minutes. Stir and cook longer if needed. To cook on the stovetop, place
the turkey (as above) in a cold, well-seasoned skillet and sauté over
medium heat for 3 to 5 minutes.

Cooking Time: 15 minutes, Yield: 4 servings

PER SERVING:
Calories 241
Protein 29 g
Carbohydrates 21 g
Fiber 7 g
Fat 5 g
Saturated Fat 2 g
Cholesterol 55 mg
Sodium 763 mg
(Analyzed without the tequila
or lime juice.)

Seafood

Seafood was not always available in the Southwest
as there is no coastline near most of the area.
Mexico, of course, is blessed with great
availability of seafood. Most of my recipes
are inspired by my numerous trips to
Mexico. Other recipes were created to take
advantage of the great compatibility of
seafood and chiles. Fresh lime is always a
wonderful accent to the chilied dishes from
the sea.

Pan Seared Tuna Steaks on Spinach a la Baja

Fresh tuna steaks are so good that they should be only subtly enhanced. This tease with orange and garlic is just perfect. Most people agree that tuna should be cooked only to the rare to medium stage to preserve the moist, fresh flavor. For this dish to be at its best, the tuna must be cut about an inch thick, no less. Wilt the fresh spinach in the same pan.

1 orange

2 cloves garlic, minced

1 tablespoon crushed caribe chile

1 tablespoon vegetable oil or oil spray (optional)

2 fresh tuna steaks (5 to 6 ounces each), cut 1 inch thick

1 10-ounce package fresh spinach, rinsed

3 tablespoons balsamic vinegar

Using a zester or a grater on the fine setting, zest the very outside (orange part only) of the orange. Squeeze the juice.

In a shallow, nonreactive bowl, combine the orange zest, juice, garlic, and caribe chile. Add the tuna and press into the liquid; turn the tuna and press the other side into the marinade. Let stand at room temperature at least 10 minutes and up to 2 hours.

About 10 minutes before serving time, heat a heavy, well-seasoned skillet until hot over medium-high heat (see Note). Remove the tuna from the marinade (reserve marinade) and cook for 4 minutes, then turn and cook for about 3 minutes. Keep warm.

Add the spinach to the skillet, drizzle with the reserved marinade, and cover. Steam for 3 to 5 minutes, until the spinach is just wilted. Add the vinegar and toss. Arrange on warm serving plates and top with the tuna.

Note: Water sprinkles should dance on the surface when it is hot enough. If you do not have a well-seasoned skillet, add 1 tablespoon vegetable oil to a skillet.

Cooking Time: 6 to 8 minutes, Yield: 2 servings

PER SERVING:
Calories 259
Protein 38 g
Carbohydrates 16 g
Fiber 4 g
Fat 8 g
Saturated Fat 2 g
Cholesterol 56 mg
Sodium 168 mg

Seared Salmon with Mango Salsa

One of the quickest, no fuss ways to prepare salmon is to simply sear it on both sides in a well-seasoned skillet. Just place a bit of salt in the skillet and shake it around and heat to medium high, then add the salmon and brown quickly on each side. Lacking a seasoned skillet, use the vegetable oil and heat until hot before adding the salmon. I think salmon is by far best if cooked only until it is still somewhat soft and shiny on the inside.

½ teaspoon salt

1 tablespoon vegetable oil (optional)

1 ½ pounds fresh salmon filet, skinned and cut into 4 3-inch-square pieces, about ½ inch thick

1 ½ cups Mango Salsa (page 172)

Sprinkle salt in a heavy, seasoned skillet and place over medium-high heat until hot. (A sprinkle of water will dance on the bottom of the pan when it is hot.) If a seasoned or nonstick pan is not available, add the oil to the pan.

Meanwhile, rinse the salmon and pat dry with a paper towel. Sauté the salmon for 3 to 5 minutes per side, until crisp and brown on the outside and still moist and bright pink on the inside. Serve with salsa.

Cooking Time: 6 to 10 minutes, Yield: 4 servings

PER SERVING:
Calories 256
Protein 34 g
Carbohydrates 2 g
Fiber 0 g
Fat 11 g
Saturated Fat 2 g
Cholesterol 96 mg
Sodium 368 mg
(Analyzed without the vegetable oil.)

Peppered Scallop Fajitas

The sweet flavor of fresh scallops really takes to the garlicky, lime-scented marinade of fajitas, and is just fabulous with a very hot 'n spicy Pico. For a leaner dish, substitute corn tortillas for the flour. 🌶

4 cloves garlic, minced
2 tablespoons freshly squeezed lime juice
1 pound bay scallops
1 medium red bell pepper, cut into ½-inch dice
4 flour tortillas
Pico de Gallo (page 174), for accompaniment

In a large bowl, combine the garlic and lime juice. Add the scallops and stir to mix well. Set aside.

In a well-seasoned skillet over medium-high heat, cook the bell pepper, stirring occasionally, until it starts to wilt and turn brown around the edges. Add the scallop mixture and cook, stirring, for 2 to 3 minutes, until the scallops are white and just cooked.

Warm the tortillas for 20 seconds, covered, in the microwave oven or briefly over a burner. Top with the scallop mixture and serve with the Pico de Gallo.

Cooking Time: 6 to 8 minutes, Yield: 4 servings

PER SERVING:
Calories 309
Protein 16 g
Carbohydrates 45 g
Fiber 3 g
Fat 7 g
Saturated Fat 1 g
Cholesterol 18 mg
Sodium 578 mg
(Analyzed without the Pico de Gallo.)

Chile-Seared Salmon with Sweet Pear Pineapple Salsa

Chiles love salmon—they add just the right accent to flavor the salmon to its greatest dimension. Fruity salsa, spiked with chiles, adds just the right complement.

1 tablespoon ground mild red chile

1 teaspoon sugar

½ teaspoon slat, plus more for sprinkling

¾ pound fresh salmon filet, deboned

1 tablespoon vegetable oil (optional)

1 cup Sweet Pear Pineapple Salsa (page 172), use about ½ recipe

In a small bowl, combine the chile, sugar, and salt. Cut the salmon into 2 pieces. Rinse, then pat dry with a paper towel. Rub the chile mixture evenly over the salmon.

Sprinkle salt in a heavy, seasoned skillet (or an unseasoned skillet to which you have added the oil). Place over medium-high heat until hot.

Sauté the salmon for 3 to 5 minutes per side, until crisp and brown on the outside and still moist and bright pink on the inside. Serve on a pool of salsa.

Cooking Time: 6 to 10 minutes, Yield: 2 servings

PER SERVING:
Calories 388
Protein 35 g
Carbohydrates 34 g
Fiber 4 g
Fat 12 g
Saturated Fat 2 g
Cholesterol 96 mg
Sodium 661 mg

Blue Corn-Crusted Red Snapper with Chipotle Cantaloupe Salsa

Blue corn is complete nutrition and was developed by the Pueblo Indians of New Mexico. It has a nuttier, stronger flavor, which is just right for the snapper. Lacking blue corn, substitute yellow or white. The Chipotle Cantaloupe Salsa is just the right flavor combination with this dish.

8 small red snapper filets (about 1 ½ pounds total)
⅓ cup blue corn flour or white or yellow cornmeal
2 to 3 tablespoons vegetable oil
Chipotle Cantaloupe Salsa (page 171)

Rinse the snapper filets and pat dry. Dust with the corn flour.
In a large, heavy skillet, heat the oil. When water dances in the skillet, add the floured filets and sauté for 5 to 6 minutes, until lightly browned. Turn and sauté the other side. Serve napped with the salsa.

Cooking Time: 10 to 12 minutes, Yield: 4 servings

PER SERVING:
Calories 254
Protein 25 g
Carbohydrates 17 g
Fiber 2 g
Fat 9 g
Saturated Fat 1 g
Cholesterol 42 mg
Sodium 58 mg

Snapper Sauced in Salsa

Down in Mexico, snapper is served many ways. This version is a quick and easy adaptation of the famous Vera Cruz-style red snapper. Serve with your favorite rice pilaf or just steamed rice. A mixed green or fresh spinach salad tartly dressed and a hard, crusty bread would be good accompaniments.

1 ½ pounds red snapper filets

⅔ cup tomato-based salsa

½ cup dry white wine

Herbed Quick Baked Potato Wedges (page 149), for accompaniment

Optional garnishes: 4 sprigs cilantro, 4 lime wedges

Rinse the snapper filets and pat dry. Place in a heavy, well-seasoned, cold sauté pan. Spread the salsa evenly over the filets.

Pour the wine into the pan, being careful not to disturb the salsa on the fish. Cover, turn to medium-high heat, and steam for 5 to 8 minutes, (turning heat down to just maintain simmer) until the fish flakes easily. Garnish with the cilantro and lime wedges, if desired. Serve with the rice or potatoes.

Cooking Time: 5 to 8 minutes, Yield: 4 servings

PER SERVING:
Calories 149
Protein 24 g
Carbohydrates 4 g
Fiber 1 g
Fat 10 g
Saturated Fat 0 g
Cholesterol 42 mg
Sodium 100 mg

Crumb-Coated Halibut with Tomatillo Salsa

Halibut is such a yummy fish! Go for the steaks, which tend to be more moist and flavorful than the filets. The crumb coating keeps all the moisture inside and is just wonderful spiced up with the Tomatillo Salsa—made extra hot.

4 halibut steaks (1-inch thick)

1 lemon, halved lengthwise

½ cup bread crumbs, preferably fresh

2 teaspoons ground pure hot red chile

2 teaspoons extra-virgin olive oil

1 cup Tomatillo Salsa, made extra hot (page 170)

Preheat the oven to 400 degrees F. Rinse the fish and pat dry, then place on an aluminum foil-covered baking sheet. Top each steak with a squeeze of lemon juice from half the lemon.

Mix the bread crumbs and chile together, then sprinkle on the top, bottom, and side of each filet. Drizzle the oil over the top of each.

Place in the oven and bake until the fish flakes easily (approximately 8 to 10 minutes) when pierced with a fork.

Cut the remaining half lemon lengthwise into quarters. Serve the fish napped with salsa and a lemon wedge.

Cooking Time: 8 to 10 minutes, Yield: 4 servings

PER SERVING:
Calories 217
Protein 38 g
Carbohydrates 4 g
Fiber 0 g
Fat 6 g
Saturated Fat 0 g
Cholesterol 57 mg
Sodium 127 mg
(Analyzed with 6 ounces halibut
steak and no Tomatillo Salsa.)

Tamale-Style Catfish

Catfish and corn are made for each other. Whether a cornmeal coating on the fish, hush puppies, or fresh corn salsa, they are all quite good together. Just for fun, I have taken the whole fresh ear of corn and stuffed the fish and salsa into the husk. Try it, you'll like it! A wonderful side dish is coleslaw made with a simple vinaigrette that is slightly sweetened.

4 ears of fresh corn or 1 15 ¼-ounce can whole kernel corn
or 1 10-ounce package frozen corn
1 4-ounce can chopped green chiles
½ cup scallions, chopped (3 or 4)
1 lime, halved lengthwise
4 catfish filets (4 to 6 ounces each)
1 teaspoon crushed red caribe chile, for garnish

Preheat the oven to 400 degrees F. If using fresh corn, carefully peel back the husk. You will use it for baking the fish. Cut the ear of corn off the stem just above the end of the cob, leaving the husk intact. Set the husk aside. Cut the corn off the cob and combine with green chiles, scallions, and the juice of half the lime.

Rinse the fish and pat dry. Place one filet inside each of the corn husks. Top each with one-fourth of the corn mixture and overlap the husks together. (If fresh corn is not available, place the fish in an oiled baking dish. Top with the corn mixture and cover.)

Bake for 12 to 15 minutes, until the fish flakes easily. Cut the remaining half lime lengthwise into 4 wedges. Serve the fish in the husk with a lime wedge on top. (Or spoon the corn out of the baking dish and place on each plate. Top with the fish and a lime wedge.)

Cooking Time: 12 to 15 minutes, Yield: 4 servings

PER SERVING:
Calories 252
Protein 22 g
Carbohydrates 23 g
Fiber 3 g
Fat 11 g
Saturated Fat 2 g
Cholesterol 54 mg
Sodium 83 mg

Vegetarian Dishes

The southwestern cuisine is made for vegetarian
dishes. The chiles marry so well with the beans,
corn, squash, and other flavors making for nutritious,
meatless foods. It can be a challenge to make sure
that meatless meals have a complete balance. After a
bit of practice, however, it can become a challenge
that is quite fun.

There are several other dishes throughout this
book that are vegetarian or can be easily altered
to become meatless.

Pasta Portobello Toss

The meaty, rich flavor of Portobello mushrooms are the best choice for this dish; however, oyster or shitake mushrooms could be substituted. Fresh mushrooms are best. Part of the mushrooms can be reconstituted dried mushrooms for a greater depth of flavor.

2 tablespoons extra-virgin olive oil, preferably Spanish

About 2 cups sliced Portobello mushrooms (1 or 2 mushrooms)

1 jalapeño, minced

8 ounces dry, uncooked spaghetti-type pasta

6 cloves garlic, minced

1 medium zucchini, unpeeled, sliced into ½-inch rounds

Boil water for the pasta. Meanwhile, in a medium skillet with deep sides, heat 1 tablespoon of the oil. Cook the mushrooms, adding the minced jalapeño. Remove the mushrooms to a bowl when soft (about 3 to 4 minutes); reserve the pan.

Cook the pasta according to package directions, adding the zucchini after 3 minutes of cooking. Drain the pasta and zucchini and add them, along with the reserved mushrooms, to the pan in which the mushrooms were cooked. Toss and serve.

Cooking Time: 8 to 10 minutes, Yield: 3 or 4 servings

PER SERVING:
(1/4 recipe)
Calories 301
Protein 9 g
Carbohydrates 49 g
Fiber 5 g
Fat 8 g
Saturated Fat 1 g
Cholesterol 0 mg
Sodium 4 mg

Hot Pasta with Broccoli

This basic recipe can be used as a guide for other vegetables such as zucchini, eggplant, asparagus, and cooked dried beans such as pinto or black. If you do not have cooked pasta at the ready, boil the water for it first and cook the broccoli in the boiling water. ♪

5 ounces dry, uncooked red or green chile fusilli pasta (4 cups cooked)

2 cups broccoli florets (2 large heads)

1 tablespoon extra-virgin olive oil, preferably Spanish

1 large onion, cut into ½-inch dice

2 large cloves garlic, minced

2 teaspoons crushed red caribe chiles

Grated Romano cheese, for garnish (optional)

If cooked pasta is not available, bring a large pot of salted water to a boil and cook the pasta according to package directions, adding the broccoli for the last five minutes. Drain and set aside. (Otherwise steam broccoli, covered, in microwave for 3 minutes.)

In a large skillet, heat the oil. Add the onion and sauté for 2 to 3 minutes, until the onion is golden. Add the garlic and cook for about 3 minutes. Add the cooked pasta and chiles and, reducing heat to medium-low, continue heating, tossing to warm evenly. Serve with the cheese, if desired.

Cooking Time: 5 minutes, Yield: 4 servings

PER SERVING:
Calories 172
Protein 6 g
Carbohydrates 29 g
Fiber 3 g
Fat 4 g
Saturated Fat 1 g
Cholesterol 0 mg
Sodium 13 mg

Southwestern Vegetable Lasagna

This dish can be varied numerous ways, substituting other vegetables, or adding more. If substituting for the refried beans, use another type of bean for nutrition's sake. Other vegetables of any kind can be used. 🌶

Nonstick oil spray

1 ½ cups tomato-based salsa

8 corn tortillas

1 15-ounce can refried pinto beans

1 10-ounce package frozen spinach, thawed

1 cup nonfat sour cream

Preheat the oven to 375 degrees F. Lightly spray an 8 x 8-inch baking dish. Spread a couple of spoonsful of salsa in the dish and top with 4 of the tortillas, arranging them in a uniform layer.

Combine the beans, spinach, and ¾ cup of the sour cream. Spread half of the mixture evenly over the tortillas. Top with half of the remaining salsa.

Arrange the remaining tortillas evenly over the bean mixture and cover with the rest of the bean mixture. Top with the balance of the salsa. Place a dollop of the reserved sour cream over the salsa. Bake for 15 to 20 minutes, until the top of the "lasagna" bubbles. Serve hot.

Cooking Time: 15 to 20 minutes, Yield: 4 servings

PER SERVING:
Calories 334
Protein 16 g
Carbohydrates 63 g
Fiber 12 g
Fat 3 g
Saturated Fat 1 g
Cholesterol 14 mg
Sodium 608 mg

Quickie Tamale Pie

This dish is the darling of the Texas one-dish dinner crowd. It is so yummy, that it has made its way across the country. Instead of slaving for hours to make it, use convenience foods such as the precooked cornmeal, often labeled polenta. This drastically reduces the preparation time, and putting it together becomes a snap. I bet meat eaters won't even miss the meat. As a variation, you can form the cornmeal into a crust by pushing it up the sides of the pan. 🌶

Nonstick oil spray

1 12-ounce package or can prepared cornmeal mush (polenta)

1 15-ounce can pinto or black beans, drained

1 15-ounce can whole kernel corn, drained

1 cup tomato-based salsa

½ cup mixed shredded Monterey Jack and Cheddar cheeses

Preheat the oven to 425 degrees F. Lightly spray an 8 x 8-inch baking dish or its equivalent. Evenly spread the cornmeal into the dish.

Combine the beans, corn, and salsa; spoon over the cornmeal. Sprinkle with the cheeses and bake for about 20 minutes, or until bubbly. Serve hot.

Cooking Time: 20 minutes, Yield: 4 servings

PER SERVING:
Calories 387
Protein 19 g
Carbohydrates 60 g
Fiber 11 g
Fat 10 g
Saturated Fat 5 g
Cholesterol 29 mg
Sodium 716 mg
(Analyzed with pinto beans.)

Pasta Toss with Seared Veggies and Black Beans

For the greatest flavor in pan-seared veggies, use a heavy, well-seasoned skillet or griddle heated to medium-high heat. Then, using no oil, cook the most liquid vegetables first, pushing them to the edges when somewhat browned. Then add the remaining veggies and sear until just browned on the outside and yet firm. 🌶

10 ounces dry, uncooked red chile rotini pasta, or plain rotini pasta and
2 tablespoons ground pure hot red chile (4 cups cooked pasta)
1 large red onion, sliced vertically into thin wedges
1 zucchini, sliced into ¼-inch thick rounds
1 red bell pepper, cut into thin strips
3 cloves garlic, minced
1 15-ounce can black beans, drained

If cooked pasta is not available, cook the pasta according to package directions. Drain and set aside.

In the meantime, in a heavy, well-seasoned skillet over medium-high heat, cook the onion, *not* stirring for a minute or two, until the edges start to brown. Stir and add zucchini, bell pepper, and garlic. Cook, stirring, until the vegetables are done.

Add the beans and heat together. Add the cooked pasta and toss together in the skillet to mix and warm evenly. Taste and adjust the seasonings. Serve hot.

Variation: For more flavor, add 1 to 2 tablespoons balsamic vinegar or red wine vinegar.

Cooking Time: 12 to 15 minutes, Yield: 4 servings

PER SERVING:
Calories 382
Protein 17 g
Carbohydrates 75 g
Fiber 12 g
Fat 2 g
Saturated Fat 0 g
Cholesterol 0 mg
Sodium 213 mg

Blackened Fresh Tomato Southwestern Pasta

Using fresh tomatoes right from the garden for this recipe (especially Romas) is always best. The secret to the special, sweet, rich flavor of this sauce is caramelizing the onions and charring the tomatoes. Oil-cured olives, beans of any kind, cubed eggplant, zucchini, or any other seasonal vegetable you have on hand, can be added.

4 Roma tomatoes, roasted under broiler until blackened (see Note)

1 onion, diced

3 cloves garlic, minced

2 dried chipotle chiles, reconstituted, and minced

½ teaspoon dried, ground, or crushed Mexican oregano

1 4-ounce can chopped green chile, drained

10 to 12 ounces dry pasta, any variety

Bring a large pot of salted water to a boil for cooking the pasta. Peel and dice the tomatoes; set aside.

In a heavy, seasoned skillet, over medium-high heat, cook the onion, not stirring for a minute or two, until the edges brown a bit, then stir and add the tomatoes. Add the garlic, chiles, and oregano. Reduce the heat to low and simmer for about 5 minutes.

Meanwhile, cook the pasta according to package directions. Drain and add to the tomato mixture. Stir together and serve.

Note: If preferred, you can blacken the tomatoes over a burner on top of the range. Frozen blackened tomatoes can also be used.

Cooking Time: 10 to 15 minutes, Yield: 4 servings

PER SERVING:
Calories 147
Protein 5 g
Carbohydrates 30 g
Fiber 3 g
Fat 1 g
Saturated Fat 0 g
Cholesterol 0 mg
Sodium 16 mg
(Analyzed with 2 ½ ounces of pasta.)

Spinach and Corn Rolled Enchiladas

These have been a hit every time I have prepared them. They are wonderfully rich and creamy and yet very healthy and not fattening. They have often been featured on the menu in restaurants for which I have consulted. 🎷

2 ears corn grilled Mexican-style (recipe page 159), or 1 10-ounce package frozen corn kernels, browned in a heavy, seasoned skillet

1 cup evaporated skim milk

3 cloves garlic, minced

Nonstick oil spray

8 corn tortillas, warmed

1 15-ounce can spinach, without salt, well drained

½ cup onion, chopped

1 cup grated low-fat Monterey Jack cheese

Cut the grilled corn from the cob, or cook frozen corn until browned. In a blender, combine the milk, garlic, and corn. Process until smooth. Transfer to a shallow plate.

Preheat the oven to 400 degrees F. Lightly spray an 8 x 8-inch baking dish with nonstick oil spray. Dip each warm tortilla in the corn mixture. Place on a flat surface and sprinkle with one-eighth of the spinach, onion, and cheese, reserving some cheese for garnish.

Roll, then place seam-side down in the baking dish. Cover with the rest of the corn mixture, making sure that you pour it evenly over each enchilada. Sprinkle with the reserved cheese. Bake for 10 minutes, or until bubbly.

Cooking Time: 20 minutes, Yield: 4 servings

PER SERVING:
Calories 330
Protein 21 g
Carbohydrates 47 g
Fiber 7 g
Fat 9 g
Saturated Fat 4 g
Cholesterol 23 mg
Sodium 413 m

Black Bean and Red Chile Flat Enchiladas

I developed this dish for a vegan vegetarian in New York City, and we both liked it so much I wanted to share it. As a vegan dish I used the fried, crispy tofu squares instead of the cheese. I know you will really like this dish.

2 cups Basic Red Chile Sauce (page 164), made with vegetable stock

8 corn tortillas, preferably blue

½ cup onion, diced medium-fine

1 15-ounce can black beans, drained

1 cup grated Cheddar cheese or 8 ounces tofu cut into ½-inch squares and crisp-fried in 1 to 2 tablespoons cooking oil

Romaine lettuce, coarsely chopped, and tomato, chopped, for garnish (optional)

Preheat the oven to 425 degrees F. Place a spoonful of sauce on 4 oven-proof plates. Top with a tortilla, then a spoonful of sauce, a layer of onion, one-eighth of the black beans, and one-eighth of the cheese. Repeat, placing a tortilla on top of the final layer of cheese.

Bake for 12 to 15 minutes, until bubbly. Serve immediately encircled with the lettuce and chopped tomato, if using.

Baking Time: 12 to 15 minutes, Yield: 4 servings

PER SERVING:
Calories 429
Protein 20 g
Carbohydrates 56 g
Fiber 14 g
Fat 15 g
Saturated Fat 8 g
Cholesterol 37 mg
Sodium 643 mg

PER SERVING:
Calories 364
Protein 20 g
Carbohydrates 56 g
Fiber 14 g
Fat 8 g
Saturated Fat 3 g
Cholesterol 14 mg
Sodium 474 mg
(Analyzed with a low-fat cheese.)

Baked Veggie Chimichangas

Chimichangas: the word literally translated means "bites for my loved one." They have been a favorite southwestern dish for several years. Originally deep-fried and smothered with sour cream, guacamole, and salsas, they taste equally good when baked and simply sauced with salsa.

1 15-ounce can pinto or black beans, well drained
1 4-ounce can diced green chiles, drained
½ cup shredded cabbage or coleslaw mix
½ cup nonfat sour cream
1 cup tomato- or tomatillo-based salsa
4 flour tortillas (10-inch size), warmed

Preheat the oven to 425 degrees F. In a medium glass bowl, combine the beans, chiles, cabbage, ¼ cup of the sour cream, and ¼ cup of the salsa. Cover and cook on high power in the microwave for 2 minutes or simmer 3 to 5 minutes in a heavy pan on top of the range.

Lay each of the warm tortillas on a baking sheet. Spoon the filling down the center of each, about 1 ½ inches in from the bottom of the tortilla and 1 inch in from each side. Bring the bottom up over the filling, tuck in each side, and roll up. Secure with toothpicks. Place seam side down on the baking sheet.

Bake for 12 to 15 minutes, until lightly browned. Remove the toothpicks and serve belted with the remaining ¾ cup salsa. Place a small dollop of the remaining sour cream in the center of each.

Cooking Time: 12 to 15 minutes, Yield: 4 servings

PER SERVING:
Calories 419
Protein 17 g
Carbohydrates 75 g
Fiber 11 g
Fat 6 g
Saturated Fat 1 g
Cholesterol 3 mg

Pizza & Pasta

Tortillas take a lot of the work out of making
pizza, as they can become instant crusts
topped with whatever chile-edged toppings
you like. I think putting chile in the sauce makes
the pizza more exciting. Another thing that makes
these pizzas fun is that you can use whatever
ingredients you like best, or have on hand, to create
the topping. For the best crust, heat the pizza in a
hot oven, under the broiler, or on top of a well-
seasoned griddle or sauté pan. Microwave ovens
do not work as well as they transfer moisture
into the crust, making it soggy.

Southwestern-spiced and flavored pastas
are great if you can find them. They are
colorful and fun for creating these pasta
dishes. If you incorporate them into the
recipe, just decrease the chile in the recipe
and check for spiciness as you add the chiles
to determine the flavor you like.

Tortilla Pizzas

These are amazingly quick to make and can be cut into pieces for an appetizer. They offer flexibility in that you can use whatever topping ingredients you have on hand. Use corn tortillas for the best nutrition; however, white or whole-wheat flour tortillas can certainly be used, if preferred.

6 corn tortillas, any kind

1 cup grated Cheddar, Monterey Jack, or mozzarella cheese

Choose 2 or more of the following: cooked pinto or black beans, drained or refried; cooked chopped beef, chicken, turkey, pork or fried crumbled chorizo; cooked crab or shrimp; small avocado, peeled and slivered; spicy salsa of your choice

Preheat the oven to 425 degrees F. Place the tortillas on a baking sheet and bake them for 6 to 8 minutes, until crisp. Divide the cheese among the tortillas. Add your choice of toppings and place back in the oven for 2 to 3 minutes, until the cheese is melted. Serve hot with additional salsa.

Cooking time: 15 minutes, Yield: 4 servings

PER SERVING:
(1/6 recipe)
Calories 115
Protein 5 g
Carbohydrates 12 g
Fiber 1 g
Fat 5 g
Saturated Fat 3 g
Cholesterol 15 mg
Sodium 130 mg
(Analyzed with one tortilla and
Cheddar cheese, toppings extra.)

Skillet Chicken Pizza

This mild-mannered pizza is at its very best when paired with a tomatillo-based salsa made as feisty as you can handle. I like to make the salsa with chipotle instead of green jalapeños for a smoky, richer flavor.

1 teaspoon olive oil or oil spray

1 ¼ cups mushrooms, sliced

½ cup onion, chopped

¼ cup white wine or chicken broth

2 cups cooked skinless chicken or turkey, chopped

2 wheat or white flour tortillas (10- to 12-inch size)

½ cup grated Monterey Jack and Cheddar cheeses, mixed

Spicy tomatillo-based salsa for garnish

Heat the oil over medium-high heat in a heavy skillet just the size of the tortillas. Add the mushrooms and onion and quickly sauté for 5 to 7 minutes, until the onion becomes clear and the mushrooms are slightly brown.

Add the wine and chicken and cook, stirring, for 3 to 5 minutes, until warm. Remove the mixture to a plate. Add a tortilla and heat for a minute or two. Add half the topping, and heat until the cheese melts. Serve with the salsa.

Cooking Time: 15 minutes, Yield: 2 servings

PER SERVING:
Calories 467
Protein 37 g
Carbohydrates 46 g
Fiber 4 g
Fat 12 g
Saturated Fat 4 g
Cholesterol 73 mg
Sodium 601 mg
(Analyzed with low-fat cheese.)

Southwestern Barbecue Pizza

Pizza is nearly everyone's quick, easy meal when there is no time or desire for cooking a complete meal. This homemade version has a thin crust due to the flour tortilla. If a thicker crust is desired, pre-made fluffy crusts are available in most supermarkets. The spice that can assist in a more healthful body comes in the form of the red chiles used in the barbecue sauce and in the caribe garnish.

2 wheat or white flour tortillas (10- to 12-inch size)

2 tablespoons spicy barbecue sauce

½ cup seared, chopped vegetables or pepperoni, cooked chicken, beef, or pork

¼ cup grated Cheddar or Monterey Jack cheeses, mixed

1 onion, chopped

Crushed red caribe chile for garnish (optional)

Preheat the oven to 425 degrees F. Place the tortillas on a baking sheet and bake for 3 minutes or until hot.

Spread half the barbecue sauce on each tortilla, then top with half the vegetables or meat. Sprinkle with half the cheeses and onion. Bake for 8 minutes, or until the cheese is bubbly. Sprinkle with the chile, if using, and serve.

Variation: Substitute the salsa for the barbecue sauce.

Cooking Time: 8 minutes, Yield: 2 servings

PER SERVING:
Calories 245
Protein 11 g
Carbohydrates 50 g
Fiber 6 g
Fat 6 g
Saturated Fat 3 g
Cholesterol 14 mg
Sodium 558 mg

Speedy Shrimp Primavera

To save time with pasta dish preparation, cook lots of pasta whenever preparing it and freeze the unused portions in meal-size quantities. The frozen pasta can be used whenever you are making one of these dishes, and voila—the meal will be done in a jiff. This is a pretty dish and can be made as hot as you like.

6 ounces dry, uncooked pasta, any type (see Note if using
    previously cooked pasta)
1 tablespoon extra-virgin olive oil
2 cloves garlic, thinly sliced
½ pound uncooked shrimp, peeled, deveined, and butterflied
¼ cup dry white wine
1 fresh jalapeño, minced or to taste
1 cup broccoli florets (1 stalk)
2 teaspoons crushed red caribe chile flakes, for garnish

Bring a large pot of salted water to a boil and cook the pasta according to package directions.

Meanwhile, heat the oil in a sauté pan, then add the garlic and cook and stir for a minute or two. Add the shrimp and cook until the pink color disappears. Add the wine, jalapeño, and about ½ cup hot water from the pasta pot. Remove from the heat and keep warm.

Two minutes before the pasta is supposed to be done, add the broccoli to the pasta pot to cook. When the pasta and broccoli are done, drain, and return them to the pot. Stir in the shrimp sauce and serve on warmed plates. Garnish with the chile flakes.

Note: If using previously cooked pasta, use hot water—it does not have to be from the pasta pot. Then, add the broccoli and cook with the shrimp. If you prefer the broccoli to be cooked more, microwave for three minutes.

Cooking Time: 15 minutes, Yield: 2 servings

PER SERVING:
Calories 521
Protein 30 g
Carbohydrates 72 g
Fiber 4 g
Fat 9 g
Saturated Fat 1 g
Cholesterol 161 mg
Sodium 200 mg
(Analyzed with low-fat cheese.)

Pasta Scramble

Because of the eggs in this dish, it is good from breakfast to dinner. It is extra-quick to prepare when the pasta is already cooked.

1 teaspoon extra-virgin olive oil, preferably Spanish

4 scallions, thinly sliced (discarding coarse green tops)

2 cloves garlic, minced

2 cups cooked pasta

4 eggs, beaten

1 jalapeño, minced

⅓ cup grated Parmesan or Romano cheese

Crushed or ground red chile, for garnish (optional)

In a large skillet over medium-high heat, warm the oil. Add the scallions, garlic, and pasta. Cook, stirring, until the pasta is lightly browned on some of the edges.

Reduce the heat to low and add the beaten eggs, jalapeño, and cheese. Stir the mixture as it cooks. When the eggs are done to your liking, serve. Sprinkle with red chile, if desired.

Cooking Time: 5 minutes, Yield: 2 servings

PER SERVING:
Calories 415
Protein 24 g
Carbohydrates 37 g
Fiber 2 g
Fat 18 g
Saturated Fat 7 g
Cholesterol 441 mg
Sodium 327 mg
(Analyzed with
Romano cheese.)

PER SERVING:
Calories 360
Protein 26 g
Carbohydrates 37 g
Fiber 2 g
Fat 12 g
Saturated Fat 4 g
Cholesterol 19 mg
Sodium 414 mg
(Analyzed with egg substitute.)

My Favorite Spicy White Clam Sauce

Easy to make and serve, this favorite sauce has been a Friday night staple since the days when we had to have something delicious, quick, and nourishing after the ride from New York City to our weekend house in Mount Tremper, outside Woodstock, New York. If fresh clams are available, select small steamers, or use canned clams. If using fresh clams, allow at least 8 ounces of clams per person. Cook them on top of the chard, as the recipe directs. ♪

6 ounces dry, uncooked linguine for 2 servings, 10 to 12 ounces for 4 servings
1 ½ tablespoons extra-virgin olive oil, preferably Spanish
4 large cloves garlic, chopped
1 bunch red Swiss chard, romaine lettuce, or spinach
2 6 ½-ounce cans chopped clams in clam juice, undrained
¼ cup white wine, preferably dry, such as Chardonnay
1 teaspoon or more crushed red pequin quebrado chile

Bring a large pot of salted water to a boil and cook the pasta according to package directions.

In a 9- to 12-inch heavy skillet over medium-high heat, warm the oil. Add the garlic and cook briefly, stirring, then add the chard. Stir and cook for 2 to 3 minutes.

Add the clams and wine and cook for 3 to 4 minutes more. Drain the pasta and serve the sauce over the hot pasta.

Cooking Time: 10 minutes, Yield: 1 to 4 servings

PER SERVING:
(1/4 recipe)
Calories 427
Protein 23 g
Carbohydrates 63 g
Fiber 7 g
Fat 8 g
Saturated Fat 1 g
Cholesterol 33 mg
Sodium 302 mg

Green Chile Cilantro Pesto

Green chiles and cilantro are naturals together in this vegetarian delight. Cilantro tames the spicy "edge" of the chiles and adds a fresh taste. The pesto is good with the addition of pan-seared scallops, shrimp, or cubed chicken breast.

10 ounces dry, uncooked angel hair pasta, vermicelli, or thin spaghetti
¼ cup low-sodium vegetable broth
1 cup green chiles, parched, peeled, and seeds removed, chopped
2 tablespoons piñons
¼ cup cilantro, including some stems, chopped
½ cup grated Romano cheese
¼ cup extra-virgin olive oil, preferably Spanish
Salt, if needed
Crushed northern New Mexican red caribe chile, for garnish (optional)

Bring a large pot of salted water to a boil and cook the pasta according to package directions.

To make the pesto, in a blender or food processor on medium speed, blend the vegetable stock, green chiles, nuts, cilantro, and cheese until just ground. Open the insert in the lid and add the oil, pouring in a fine stream. Continue blending until all the oil has been incorporated.

Taste the pesto and add salt, if desired. Drain the pasta and divide among the plates. Top each serving with the pesto. Garnish with the caribe chile, if desired.

Cooking Time: 10 minutes, Yield: 4 servings

PER SERVING:
Calories 427
Protein 24 g
Carbohydrates 63 g
Fiber 7 g
Fat 8 g
Saturated Fat 1 g
Cholesterol 33 mg
Sodium 302 mg

Chipotle Salsa Tossed with Pasta

This recipe is a takeoff on puttanesca sauce and is so wonderful atop pasta. Chipotles are the red, ripe jalapeños that have been smoked and are a wonderful complement to the olives and bacon. ♪

10 ounces dry, uncooked pasta, any kind

2 cups chipotle salsa, or 1 ¾ cups tomato-based salsa
with ¼ cup minced reconstituted chipotles (page 62)

½ cup Mediterranean-type olives, sliced in strips, pits removed

¼ pound bacon, fried, drained, and crumbled

¼ cup cilantro, coarsely chopped

Grated Romano or Parmesan cheese, for garnish (optional)

Bring a large pot of salted water to a boil and cook the pasta according to package directions.

Meanwhile, in a small pan, combine the salsa, olives, bacon, and cilantro. Simmer for 5 minutes to blend the flavors. When the pasta is done, drain and divide among the plates. Top each with the salsa. Sprinkle with cheese, if desired.

Cooking Time: 10 to 12 minutes, Yield: 2 large or 4 small servings

PER SERVING:
(1/4 recipe)
Calories 382
Protein 18 g
Carbohydrates 65 g
Fiber 8 g
Fat 6 g
Saturated Fat 1 g
Cholesterol 16 mg
Sodium 923 mg
(Analyzed with
Canadian bacon.)

PER SERVING:
(1/4 recipe)
Calories 383
Protein 14 g
Carbohydrates 64 g
Fiber 8 g
Fat 8 g
Saturated Fat 2 g
Cholesterol 8 mg
Sodium 634 mg
(Analyzed with regular bacon.)

Soup

I can remember as a child, when visiting my aunt
and uncle who lived in Oaxaca, Mexico, how they
started every noon meal with a sopa, or soup.
Their wonderful, freshly-made soups were often
flavored with chiles and were usually broth-based.
I developed many of these soups borrowing from
this taste memory. Corn tortillas are a popular
thickener and are ever present. When they simmer
and break down, after a few moments of cooking,
the resulting soup has a marvelous flavor and a
texture approaching that of a chowder.

Try fresh corn or wheat-flour tortillas as
an accompaniment to these soups instead
of crackers or bread. Corn tortillas are
especially healthy for you. If the tortillas
are not fresh, cut them into thin strips,
which I call shoestrings, bake them until
crisp, and scatter them over any bowl of
soup. (Follow the recipe for preparing them
on page 36.)

Speedy Chili

This is quite a respectable chili; however, it's not the original Bowl o' Red, my favorite. This version is made with ground beef to speed up the cooking time, whereas the "Bowl" recipe is made with hand cut cubes of chuck, requiring much longer cooking. Making lots of chili at a time is always a good idea as it really does improve with age. Serve with coarsely shredded Cheddar and Monterey Jack cheeses mixed, pickled jalapeños, chopped onion, and sour cream with lime wedges laced with red chile. This chili, with so much of all the natural oxidative power of red chile, will actually freeze quite well for a year. 🌶

1 pound ground chuck (80 percent lean)
½ cup onion, chopped (½-inch dice)
2 cloves garlic, minced
3 tablespoons freshly ground pure mild red New Mexican chile
1 14 ½-ounce can water-packed stewed tomatoes, diced
1 teaspoon freshly ground cumin, or to taste
½ teaspoon salt, or to taste
1 15-ounce can pinto beans (optional)

PER SERVING:
Calories 261
Protein 21 g
Carbohydrates 11 g
Fiber 3 g
Fat 15 g
Saturated Fat 6 g
Cholesterol 72 mg
Sodium 592 mg
(Analyzed without beans and with 80 percent lean ground beef.)

PER SERVING:
Calories 352
Protein 27 g
Carbohydrates 28 g
Fiber 8 g
Fat 16 g
Saturated Fat 6 g
Cholesterol 72 mg
Sodium 904 mg
(Analyzed with beans and 80 percent lean ground beef.)

Crumble the meat into a heavy, 5-quart Dutch oven-type pot. Sauté over medium heat until the pink color disappears. Tilt the pot and spoon out any visible fat. Add the onion and garlic to the pot and continue simmering for 3 to 5 minutes, until the onion becomes soft and clear.

Remove the pot from the heat and stir in the chile, tomatoes, cumin, and salt. Add the beans, if using (see Note). Return to the heat and simmer for another 10 to 15 minutes. Taste and adjust the seasonings. If time allows, refrigerate for a day or two so the flavors can develop. If not, serve immediately.

Note: Many Western chili buffs prefer to cook the chili and beans separately, then serve the beans on the bottom of the bowl, topped with the chili.

Preparation Time: 20 minutes, Yield: 4 servings

Chipotle-Teased Black Bean Pumpkin Soup

The smoky heat of the chipotles adds a spark to the hearty goodness of black beans. Pumpkin or any winter squash is a wonderful complement to black beans. I make spicy black bean soup and butternut squash soup and purée each separately. To serve, I pour them simultaneously into each bowl. This one soup captures these twin flavors quickly and easily.

1 15-ounce can black beans, undrained
1 14 ½-ounce can chicken broth, preferably low sodium
1 cup onion, chopped (1 large onion)
1 dried chipotle chile, reconstituted and minced (page 62)
1 15-ounce can pumpkin
1 to 2 teaspoons ground cumin
Salt (optional)
Optional garnishes: 2 tablespoons sour cream, 1 lime cut into wedges

In a heavy, 3-quart saucepan, combine the beans, broth, onion, chile, and pumpkin; bring to a simmer and cook for about 10 minutes, or until the onion softens.

Transfer the mixture to a blender or food processor and whirl until thick and smooth. Return to the pan and add 1 teaspoon of the cumin; taste to determine if you desire the remaining cumin or salt.

Serve in bowls. If desired, garnish with a squeeze of lime, a dollop of sour cream, and a sprig of cilantro.

Cooking Time: 20 minutes, Yield: 2 large or 4 small servings

PER SERVING:
(1/4 recipe)
Calories 143
Protein 9 g
Carbohydrates 26 g
Fiber 10 g
Fat 2 g
Saturated Fat 1 g
Cholesterol 2 mg
Sodium 381 mg

Chile-Sparked Sweet Potato Soup

This soup seems quite hearty and has a wonderful flavor, yet a serving has fewer than 150 calories. I particularly like the topping of crispy, crunchy tortilla shoestrings, which are very thinly cut and toasted corn tortillas (page 36).

2 medium sweet potatoes, peeled and cut into ½-inch dice
4 scallions, thinly sliced (1 tablespoon sliced tops reserved for garnish)
1 cup evaporated skim milk
1 tablespoon ground pure hot red chile, or to taste
Few grates of fresh nutmeg
Baked tortilla shoestrings for garnish (page 36)

Place the potatoes, scallions, and 1 cup water in a 2-quart glass or microwavable plastic bowl. Cover with plastic wrap and microwave on full power for 10 minutes (see Note).

Transfer the potato mixture to a food processor. Add the milk and 2 teaspoons of the chile and process until puréed. Stir in the nutmeg. Return to the 2-quart container and microwave for about 2 minutes, or until hot.

Serve each bowl garnished with the reserved chile, scallion, and corn tortilla.

Note: To cook conventionally, place the sweet potatoes, 1 cup water, and scallions in a heavy, medium saucepan, cover, and simmer for about 15 minutes, or until fork-tender. Purée as above, and heat to serving temperature.

Cooking Time: 12 minutes in a microwave oven, 20-30 minutes in a conventional oven,
Yield: 4 servings

PER SERVING:
Calories 142
Protein 6 g
Carbohydrates 28 g
Fiber 3 g
Fat 1 g
Saturated Fat 0 g
Cholesterol 2 mg
Sodium 86 mg

Pumpkin Pinto Bisque

This soup is historic, combining two of the ages-old staples of the Pueblo Indians—squash and corn. Squash of all types grows wild along the irrigation ditches in the Southwest. In this case, the squash is pumpkin, a variation. Pinto beans, the healthiest of all beans, pairs tastefully with the pumpkin in this very quick-to-make soup. Canned ingredients really speed up the preparation.

1 cup onion, diced (1 large onion), 4 teaspoons reserved for garnish
1 15 ½-ounce can pinto beans, undrained
1 15 ½-ounce can pumpkin
½ teaspoon salt, or to taste
1 12-ounce can evaporated skim milk
1 tablespoon ground pure hot red chile, or to taste, plus more for garnish

Place the onion in a heavy, nonstick pan with a close-fitting cover. Cook over medium heat for 3 to 4 minutes, until the onion becomes clear.

Add the beans, pumpkin, salt, milk, and chile. Reduce the heat to low and simmer for 10 to 15 minutes, until the flavors blend. Serve in large bowls topped with a sprinkle of chile and the reserved onion.

Cooking Time: 15 to 20 minutes, Yield: 4 servings

PER SERVING:
Calories 221
Protein 14 g
Carbohydrates 40 g
Fiber 9 g
Fat 2 g
Cholesterol 3 mg
Sodium 732 mg

Fall Harvest Soup

You could call this Jack-o-lantern soup and use the leftover pumpkin from the Jack-o-lantern if you wish. Canned pumpkin of course is easier. If at all possible, use fresh sage. (It is a great perennial, by the way. Once you plant it, you will always have it.)

1 15-ounce can pumpkin

6 to 8 fresh sage leaves or ½ teaspoon ground dried sage, 1 to 4 leaves reserved for garnish

½ teaspoon salt

Several grinds of black pepper

2 teaspoons ground pure hot red New Mexican chile

1 onion, chopped

2 cloves garlic, minced

1 5-ounce can evaporated skim milk

In a heavy, 3-quart saucepan, combine the pumpkin, sage, salt, pepper, chile, onion, and garlic. Rinse out the pumpkin can with 1 cup water and add to the pan. Bring to a simmer and cook for 15 minutes.

Transfer the mixture to a food processor or blender and process until smooth. Add the milk, return the mixture to the pan, and cook for 3 to 5 minutes to blend the flavors. Taste and adjust the seasonings. Serve in warm soup bowls garnished with the sage leaves or a dash of ground sage.

Cooking Time: 20 minutes, Yield: 2 large or 4 small servings

PER SERVING:
(1/4 recipe)
Calories 84
Protein 5 g
Carbohydrates 17 g
Fiber 4 g
Fat 1 g
Saturated Fat 0 g
Cholesterol 1 mg
Sodium 344 mg

Southwestern Chicken Vegetable Soup

Made from grilled chicken, perhaps left over from a previous grilled dinner, this soup is quick to prepare. Summer calabacitas or zucchini give it a fresh flavor.

1 14 ½-ounce can chicken broth, preferably low sodium

1 cup grilled chicken, cubed in ½-inch dice

1 large tomato, cut into 1-inch chunks

1 small zucchini, thinly sliced

1 jalapeño, minced

2 large cloves garlic, minced

About ½ teaspoon crushed caribe chile, for garnish (optional)

In a heavy, 3-quart saucepan, combine the broth, chicken, tomato, zucchini, jalapeño, and garlic. Simmer for about 15 minutes. Serve warm. For a colorful garnish, dust with the caribe chile.

Cooking Time: 15 minutes, Yield: 2 large or 4 small servings

PER SERVING:
(1/4 recipe)
Calories 86
Protein 13 g
Carbohydrates 4 g
Fiber 1 g
Fat 3 g
Saturated Fat 1 g
Cholesterol 32 mg
Sodium 78 mg

Green Chile Corn Chowder

If possible, use grilled fresh corn—grilled whole on the cob. Canned corn will work, but it will not be as highly flavored. 𝄞

1 15 ¼-ounce can whole kernel corn
1 14 ½-ounce can chicken broth, preferably low sodium
½ cup onion, diced
1 4-ounce can diced green chiles
1 tomato, diced
Corn chips, for garnish (optional)

In a heavy, 3-quart saucepan, combine the corn, broth, onion, chiles, and tomato. Simmer uncovered for 15 minutes. Taste and adjust the seasonings. Serve in warm bowls with a few corn chips on top of each.

Cooking Time: 15 minutes, Yield: 2 large or 4 small servings

PER SERVING:
(1/4 recipe)
Calories 99
Protein 4 g
Carbohydrates 22 g
Fiber 3 g
Fat 2 g
Saturated Fat 1 g
Cholesterol 2 mg
Sodium 613 mg

Chicken Tortilla Chowder

As mentioned earlier, this is a favorite of Wendy's, who has worked with me for several years. In our week-long Advanced Cooking School, we pair this soup with a "made from scratch" creamy green chile chicken soup. Frequently, most find the flavor of this soup preferable over the longer to prepare, higher calorie version. This soup really makes a meal when accompanied by a simple fresh vegetable or fruit salad.

1 14 ½-ounce can chicken broth, with water added to make 2 cups

2 white or yellow corn tortillas, broken up

1 pound chicken breasts, trimmed and cut into 1-inch cubes

3 scallions, thinly sliced (some reserved for garnish)

1 ½ tablespoons minced pickled jalapeños with juice

Optional garnishes: cilantro leaves, crushed red caribe chiles, lime wedges

Place the chicken broth and water in a 3-quart saucepan over medium heat. Add the tortillas and chicken. Cover, reduce the heat to low, and simmer stirring, for 5 to 6 minutes.

Add the scallions and jalapeños with juice. Stir to combine well. Simmer for about another 5 minutes. Serve garnished with the reserved scallion and, if desired, the cilantro, chiles, and lime to squeeze on the chowder.

Cooking Time: 10 to 12 minutes, Yield: 2 servings

PER SERVING:
Calories 326
Protein 50 g
Carbohydrates 14 g
Fiber 2 g
Fat 8 g
Saturated Fat 2 g
Cholesterol 130 mg
Sodium 338 mg

Wraps

Wraps have always been "in" in southwestern and Mexican food. With tortilla-wrapped favorites such as tacos, enchiladas, burritos, chimichangas, and fajitas, to name just a few, you can easily see that this trend is not new. It's just been a fusion of the always-popular southwestern dishes and other American favorites.

Each of these recipes is trimmer than usual, offering low-fat and healthy alternatives. Remember that you can eliminate quite a few calories by reaching for corn rather than wheat tortillas. For an especially low-fat dish, try Swiss Chard Wrapped Salmon (page 141). Rockefeller Roll-Ups (page 135) and Texas Veggie Hash Burritos (page 138) are both vegetarian dishes.

Speedy Enchiladas

Enchiladas are traditionally the favorite main dish with native New Mexicans. And the hotter, the better. Newcomers or tourists to the state tend to like the green chile chicken enchiladas the best, and longtime residents tend to prefer the red chile beef.

2 cups Basic Red Chile Sauce (page 164) or Favorite Green Chile Sauce (page 165)

8 corn tortillas

1 ½ cups cooked chicken or beef, shredded

¾ cup Monterey Jack or Cheddar cheese, coarsely grated, plus ¼ cup for garnish

½ cup onion, chopped (1 small onion)

4 leaves romaine lettuce, sliced into 1-inch-wide ribbons, for garnish (optional)

Heat the chile sauce for about 2 minutes in the microwave oven or 5 to 6 minutes on top of the range. Keep warm. Heat the tortillas in a plastic bag in the microwave oven for 1 minute at full power or wrapped in aluminum foil for 5 to 10 minutes in a 400 degree F. oven. (Leave the oven on for warming the enchiladas.)

Place the tortillas on 4 microwave-safe or ovenproof plates. Place a spoonful of the chile sauce down the center of each tortilla. Divide the meat among the tortillas. Top with the cheese and onion. Roll up each tortilla, then place seam side down on the plates. Drizzle with the remaining sauce and sprinkle with the reserved cheese. Place in the microwave oven for a minute each or in the conventional oven for 5 to 8 minutes.

Preparation Time: 8 minutes in a microwave oven, 20 minutes in a conventional oven, Yield: 4 servings

PER SERVING:
Calories 409
Protein 29 g
Carbohydrates 38 g
Fiber 7 g
Fat 17 g
Saturated Fat 8 g
Cholesterol 80 mg
Sodium 650 mg

PER SERVING:
Calories 364
Protein 30 g
Carbohydrates 38 g
Fiber 7 g
Fat 11 g
Saturated Fat 5 g
Cholesterol 66 mg
Sodium 684 mg
(Analyzed with low-fat cheese.)

Rockefeller Roll-ups

Healthy and lean, yet rich enough to be sinful, these fun-to-make vegetarian wraps are good as a snack or a light meal when cut into small appetizer-size servings. 🌶

1 12-ounce package fresh spinach

6 ounces (¾ cup) nonfat cream cheese or goat cheese, at room temperature

1 tablespoon crushed red caribe chiles, plus 1 tablespoon for garnish

1 15-ounce can refried black or pinto beans

8 tablespoons (½ cup) red or green salsa

4 wheat-flour tortillas (8-inch size)

Rinse the spinach and dry well. Chop about a fourth of it into ½-inch pieces. Reserve the remaining spinach.

Combine the chopped spinach with the cream cheese and 1 tablespoon of the chiles.

Place the beans in a small bowl, cover with plastic wrap, and warm in the microwave oven for 2 minutes on full power.

To assemble the roll-ups, lay the tortillas on a flat surface. Spread each with one-fourth of the cream cheese mixture and the beans. Place 2 tablespoons of the salsa down the center of each and roll up. Then arrange the reserved spinach leaves on 4 plates. Place the roll-ups on the plates (or eat them out of hand and reserve the spinach for later use) and sprinkle with the reserved chiles, scattering them over the plates to create a confetti effect.

Preparation Time: 10 to 15 minutes, Yield: 4 servings

PER SERVING:
Calories 337
Protein 20 g
Carbohydrates 53 g
Fiber 11 g
Fat 6 g
Saturated Fat 2 g
Cholesterol 12 mg
Sodium 888 mg

Chevre Wrap

I created this dish for a light luncheon, while consulting for Conrad's restaurant, named for Conrad Hilton, the former owner of the historic landmark hotel where our cooking school is located. To display them attractively, I make every other cut on an angle and then arrange the longer angular side of each cut toward the outside and arrange them in fours, making them look like flowers, especially when centering each "flower" with a piece of tomato. ∬

1 spinach or sun-dried tomato wheat tortilla (12-inch size)
2 tablespoons low-fat or nonfat herbed chevre
2 tablespoons Hot New Mexican Table Salsa (page 160)
½ cup loosely packed mesclun salad greens
1 tablespoon Cilantro Pesto (page 106)
Optional garnishes: 1 tablespoon chopped tomato, 1 teaspoon piñon,
Tomatillo Salsa (page 162)

Lay the tortilla flat. Spread with the cheese followed by the salsa, greens, and pesto. Roll tightly. Cut and arrange as stated above. Garnish.

Preparation Time: 3 to 5 minutes, Yield: 1 large serving or 12 appetizers

PER SERVING:
(full recipe)
Calories 417
Protein 15 g
Carbohydrates 61 g
Fiber 5 g
Fat 12 g
Saturated Fat 2 g
Cholesterol 4 mg
Sodium 708 mg

Texas Veggie Hash Burritos

This veggie hash could also serve as a nest for baked or poached eggs topped with salsa. Corn tortillas are much less caloric and more nutritious than the flour. Have fun with this!

2 large baking potatoes, unpeeled and diced

2 medium zucchini, unpeeled and diced

1 small onion, diced

2 cloves garlic, minced

1 4-ounce can green chiles, undrained, or ½ cup parched, peeled, and chopped

4 10- to 12-inch flour tortillas or 8 6-inch corn tortillas

Optional garnishes: salsa, cheeses, or sour cream

Place the potatoes, zucchini, onion, and garlic in a 2-quart microwave-safe bowl (see Note). Add ½ cup water, cover with a lid or plastic wrap, and cook in the microwave oven on full power for 5 minutes, or until fork-tender. Stir and add the chiles and their liquid. Taste the vegetable mixture and add salt, if desired.

Heat the tortillas. Place the vegetable mixture on each tortilla, leaving a 1-inch margin. Fold the bottom 1 inch up around the filling, then roll up the tortilla. Serve with garnish, if desired.

Note: If cooking conventionally, simmer vegetables in an inch of water for 12 to 15 minutes until done. Add drained chiles.

Cooking Time: 5 minutes in a microwave oven, 15 minutes conventionally,
Yield: 4 servings

PER SERVING:
Calories 332
Protein 9 g
Carbohydrates 63 g
Fiber 5 g
Fat 5 g
Saturated Fat 1 g
Cholesterol 0 mg
Sodium 352 mg
(Analyzed with flour tortillas and no optional ingredients.)

Shrimp Salad Burrito

Seafood and rice have always been a popular combination. Add the crunch of your favorite salad greens and spicy salsa and you have a quick, sure winner. For speed's sake, prepare the rice ahead. Cooked rice keeps several days in the refrigerator or in the freezer for up to ninety days. 🌶

4 10-inch wheat-flour tortillas or 8 corn tortillas
1 cup cooked white rice, at room temperature
2 cups mixed lettuces, rinsed and spun dry
¾ pound cooked bay or baby shrimp, peeled, deveined, and chilled
¼ cup Hot New Mexican Table Salsa, (page 168) plus more for garnish

Warm the tortillas either in a plastic bag in the microwave oven for 1 minute, individually over a burner for a few seconds per side, or wrapped in aluminum foil in a 350 degree F. oven for about 10 minutes.

Place the tortillas on a flat work surface. Place a 2-inch-wide strip of rice down the center of each tortilla, leaving about a 1 ½-inch margin at one end.

Place the lettuce on top of the rice, then top with the shrimp and salsa. Fold the 1 ½-inch margin up over the filling, then roll the tortilla. Serve immediately with more salsa.

Preparation Time: 3 minutes, Yield: 4 servings

PER SERVING:
Calories 380
Protein 26 g
Carbohydrates 53 g
Fiber 3 g
Fat 6 g
Saturated Fat 1 g
Cholesterol 166 mg
Sodium 559 mg
(Analyzed with plain rice and
Hot New Mexican Table Salsa.)

Crab Chard Wraps

Crab is so flavorful, it does not need much embellishment other than some hot chile and perhaps a squish of lime or lemon. Here, scallions and the mild flavor of pasta add texture and taste. These ingredients also serve to stretch the crab for stuffing into a steamed chard leaf. The mixture could also be stuffed it into a corn tortilla, if you wish to eat out of hand.

4 large leaves red-veined Swiss chard, well rinsed
½ pound cooked crab or surimi (imitation crab)
1 tablespoon freshly squeezed lime juice
4 scallions, including tender green parts, chopped
2 cups cooked pasta, such as fusilli, or cooked rice
Jalapeño Lime Cream Dressing (page 167), for garnish (optional)

Place the chard leaves in a plastic bag or a bowl, cover with plastic wrap, and cook in the microwave oven on high power for about 1 minute, or until the leaves wilt. Or drop the leaves into rapidly boiling water and cook conventionally for about 2 minutes.

Combine the crab, lime juice, scallions, and pasta. Taste and add seasonings, if desired. Divide the crab mixture among the leaves; roll up and secure each with a toothpick.

To eat out of hand, enclose each wrap in a corn tortilla that has been warmed in a plastic bag in the microwave oven for 20 seconds or over a burner just until warm. If desired, serve napped with the Jalapeño Lime Cream Dressing.

Preparation Time: 5 to 7 minutes, Yield: 4 servings

PER SERVING:
Calories 171
Protein 16 g
Carbohydrates 23 g
Fiber 2 g
Fat 2 g
Saturated Fat 0 g
Cholesterol 57 mg
Sodium 263 mg

Swiss Chard Wrapped Salmon

Chard, especially the red-veined variety, looks pretty wrapped around the salmon. The leaves are generally so big that you will not have any trouble tucking the sides and stem under the salmon. Do not trim off the stem; it makes a great looking belt around the salmon. 🌶

4 large leaves Swiss chard, well rinsed

1 pound salmon filet or steak, bones removed

4 teaspoons minced reconstituted chipotle chiles (page 62)

1 lime, cut into 8 slices

Place the chard leaves in a plastic bag and cook on high in the microwave oven for about 1 minute, or until they wilt. Or immerse the leaves in rapidly boiling water for about 2 minutes.

Drain the leaves and lay them flat on a work surface. Cut the salmon into 4 equal portions and place one on each leaf.

Place 1 teaspoon chipotles on each filet and spread as uniformly as possible. Top each filet with 2 slices of lime. Wrap the chard leaf around the fillings and secure with toothpicks, if needed.

Place the salmon wraps on a microwave-safe plate, cover with plastic wrap, and cook in the microwave oven on high power for 2 to 3 minutes, until done (see Note). The thinner the cut of salmon, the faster it will cook. The salmon should be somewhat shiny in the center for the best flavor. Serve hot.

Note: To cook the salmon conventionally, preheat the oven to 425 degrees F. Place the wraps on a baking sheet and cover with aluminum foil. Cook for 10 minutes.

Cooking Time: 3 to 4 minutes in a microwave oven, Yield: 4 servings

PER SERVING:
Calories 182
Protein 22 g
Carbohydrates 3 g
Fiber 1 g
Fat 9 g
Saturated Fat 2 g
Cholesterol 68 mg
Sodium 155 mg

Cumin Chicken Chimi with Cilantro Orange Sauce

The heady scent of freshly ground cumin crosses many cultures but is particularly good in southwestern dishes. A must in chili con carne, it is equally appropriate with this wonderful chicken filling. I have taken liberties calling this a chimi. It is not baked or fried.

CHIMI

1 pound boneless, skinless chicken breasts or thighs

1 orange

3 cloves garlic

1 ½ teaspoons freshly ground cumin

½ teaspoon crushed pequin quebrado or other hot red chile

8 corn tortillas

Cilantro Orange Sauce

CILANTRO ORANGE SAUCE

Remaining orange zest

½ cup plain yoghurt

About 1 tablespoon chopped cilantro

Trim the chicken of any excess fat and connective tissue and cut the meat into 1-inch chunks. Using a zester, remove the orange zest and juice the orange. In a large bowl, combine the orange juice, about 1 teaspoon of the zest, the garlic, cumin, and chile. Add the chicken and stir to mix well. Allow to sit in the marinade for at least 10 minutes—30 minutes is even better. Drain.

In a heavy, well-seasoned skillet over medium-high heat, brown the drained chicken for 2 to 3 minutes. Turn and brown the other side. Meanwhile, warm the tortillas in a plastic bag in the microwave oven for 1 minute, or individually over a burner for a few seconds per side, or wrapped in aluminum foil in a 425 degree F. oven for about 5 minutes or until hot and pliable.

To make the sauce: Combine zest, yoghurt, and cilantro; mix well. Divide the chicken among the tortillas, roll up the tortillas, and place seam side down on serving plates. Nap with Cilantro Orange Sauce, if desired.

Cooking Time: 8 to 10 minutes, Yield: 4 servings

PER SERVING:
Calories 258
Protein 26 g
Carbohydrates 29 g
Fiber 3 g
Fat 4 g
Saturated Fat 1 g
Cholesterol 63 mg
Sodium 141 mg
(Analyzed with chicken breast.)

Grilled Lamb Soft Tacos

I will always remember how much Kathie Lee Gifford and Regis Filbin liked this dish when I prepared it on their television show. Kathie Lee in particular kept coming back for more. The fresh garlic, ginger, and jalapeño jelly really complement the succulent lamb. And, the Cilantro Salsa just completes the picture. The lamb is best grilled, even if it is an inside, stovetop grill. ♪

1 pound trimmed boneless leg of lamb, or sirloin steaks

3 cloves garlic, minced

1 ½-inch piece fresh ginger, peeled and minced

½ cup mild jalapeño jelly or jam (see Note)

4 flour tortillas (8- to 10-inch size)

Cilantro Salsa (page 173), for garnish (optional)

Cut the lamb into ½-inch slices; set aside. Combine the garlic, ginger, and jelly. Spread the ginger mixture on each slice of lamb.

Meanwhile, preheat an outdoor grill, stovetop grill, or a heavy, seasoned skillet to medium-high heat.

To cook, separate the lamb slices and place them on the grill or in the skillet; sear for 2 to 3 minutes per side, until medium rare. Meanwhile, warm the tortillas in a plastic bag for 1 minute or briefly over a burner. Divide the filling among the tortillas, and wrap each tortilla around the filling. Serve with a bowl of the salsa, if desired.

Note: Warm the jelly in a microwave oven for 30 seconds, or in a boiling water bath, until it liquefies.

Cooking Time: 4 to 6 minutes, Yield: 4 servings

PER SERVING:
Calories 501
Protein 30 g
Carbohydrates 69 g
Fiber 3 g
Fat 12 g
Saturated Fat 4 g
Cholesterol 73 mg
Sodium 415 mg
(Analyzed with 10-inch tortillas.)

Breakfast Wrap

Charles Moore, a favorite alumnus who attended both a weeklong and a weekend class in our cooking school, shared this with us. It is a quick snack for most any time of day or a nourishing breakfast, if you must be on the run. ♪

2 eggs
2 tablespoons bacon bits or bacon-flavored soy texturized protein bits
3 stuffed green olives, sliced
1 fresh or pickled jalapeño, minced
½ teaspoon Pecos Valley Spice Co. ground pure mild red chile powder
Nonstick oil spray
1 flour tortilla (8-inch size)

Crack the eggs into a small bowl and whip. Add the bacon bits, olives, jalapeño, and chile powder and whisk again.

Lightly spray a heavy, well-seasoned skillet with nonstick oil spray and place over medium-low heat. Add the egg mixture and cook, stirring, until it is as firm as you like. Heat the tortilla briefly over the burner you were cooking on. Place the egg mixture in the center of the tortilla and roll it up. Serve immediately.

Cooking Time: 2 to 3 minutes, Yield: 1 serving

PER SERVING:
Calories 501
Protein 30 g
Carbohydrates 69 g
Fiber 3 g
Fat 12 g
Saturated Fat 4 g
Cholesterol 73 mg
Sodium 415 mg
(Analyzed with 10-inch tortillas.)

Fajita Favorites

Fajitas are at their best when made simply—by marinating the meat in freshly-squeezed lime juice, garlic, a little oil, and ground black pepper.

Another secret is to never slice the meat until after it is cooked. Fajitas prepared this way will be juicy and flavorful instead of dried out and dull. For convenience, I like to make lots of fajita filling at once and freeze it in one-serving portions. Although the original fajita was made with skirt steak, I like to make all kinds—including beef (see lamb recipe, page 66), chicken, turkey, duck, shrimp, and scallops.

> 1 ½ pounds lean, trimmed skirt steak; boneless, skinless chicken breast; or peeled, deveined, uncooked shrimp
>
> ¼ cup freshly-squeezed lime juice (2 or 3 limes)
>
> 4 cloves garlic, minced
>
> 2 tablespoons vegetable oil or extra-virgin olive oil, preferably Spanish
>
> Several grinds of black pepper (optional)
>
> 4 flour tortillas (6- to 8-inch size), warmed
>
> Grilled or pan-seared onion and bell pepper slices, Pico de Gallo (page 174), and sour cream, for garnish (optional)

Trim the beef or chicken. Pound the beef with a tenderizer mallet. Flatten the chicken with a French tenderizer-pounder or the side of a chef's knife or cleaver.

In a shallow bowl, mix the lime juice, garlic, oil, and black pepper, if using. Allow to marinate about 10 minutes. If not cooking immediately, freeze in individual plastic bags.

Meanwhile, preheat the grill. Cook the beef for about 3 minutes per side, or until rare. Cook the chicken for about 4 minutes per side. Cook the shrimp for about 2 minutes per side, or until the shrimp turn pink. Slice the beef or chicken across the grain into ½-inch-wide strips.

Place the beef, chicken, or shrimp in each warm tortilla. Top with the grilled bell peppers and onions, if using, and roll up the tortillas. Serve with the Pico de Gallo and sour cream, if desired.

Cooking Time: 4 to 8 minutes, Yield: 4 servings

PER SERVING:
(beef fajitas)
Calories 446
Protein 40 g
Carbohydrates 28 g
Fiber 2 g
Fat 18 g
Saturated Fat 7 g
Cholesterol 88 mg
Sodium 341 mg
(Note: The fat can be trimmed with leaner meat, such as sirloin tip or chicken.)

PER SERVING:
(chicken fajitas)
Calories 358
Protein 39 g
Carbohydrates 28 g
Fiber 2 g
Fat 9 g
Saturated Fat 2 g
Cholesterol 94 mg
Sodium 314 mg

PER SERVING:
(shrimp fajitas)
Calories 298
Protein 30 g
Carbohydrates 28 g
Fiber 2 g
Fat 6 g
Saturated Fat 1 g
Cholesterol 242 mg
Sodium 511 mg

Meal Complements

You can definitely prepare more exciting
southwestern vegetables than the predictable
beans and rice so often served in southwestern
or Mexican restaurants. Chile pairs beautifully
with vegetables. The starchier types, such as
potatoes, really take on chiles well—actually they
are first cousins.

Some of the vegetables that I have included are
not predictable southwestern vegetables, such as
kale; however, it is the healthiest of all greens
and definitely worth including.

For a different taste treat, try the Salsa Verde
Rice or Green Chile Cheese Rice—or the
Grilled Corn recipe with one of the toppings.

Chipotle and Roasted Garlic Mashed Potatoes

The rich flavors of the chipotle chiles overlaced with the roasted garlic are wonderful in mashed potatoes. Infusing the potatoes with butter makes for a rich flavor. 🌶

¾ teaspoon salt

4 pounds russet, golden, or baking potatoes, peeled and quartered

1 ½ tablespoons unsalted butter

½ head garlic, roasted (see Note)

¾ cup milk (skim for lowest fat or evaporated skim for a richer flavor)

2 dried chipotle chiles, reconstituted (page 62), minced

Bring about an inch of salted water to a boil. Add the potatoes, cover, and cook for about 15 minutes, or until the potatoes are tender.

Drain well, then add the butter. Cover and let stand while preparing the garlic.

Slice off the root end of the roasted garlic. With the blunt edge of a knife, squeeze the garlic from the husk; mince and set aside.

Warm the milk for about 30 seconds. Mash the potatoes using a masher, slowly adding milk and mashing until the potatoes are fluffy. Fold in the minced chiles and garlic. Serve hot.

Note: To roast garlic, lightly oil the head, then cover with foil or place in a garlic baker (lots of garlic can be done at once). Bake in the oven at 400 degrees F. for 20 to 30 minutes or until soft to the touch when pressed.

Cooking Time: 15 minutes, Yield: 8 servings

PER SERVING:
Calories 204
Protein 4 g
Carbohydrates 42 g
Fiber 4 g
Fat 2 g
Saturated Fat 1 g
Cholesterol 6 mg
Sodium 241 mg
(Analyzed with skim milk.)

Herbed, Quick-Baked Potato Wedges

This is one of my very favorite ways to prepare potatoes. Be sure to use a waxy new potato, such as the red or gold ones.

4 medium potatoes

1 tablespoon extra-virgin olive oil, preferably Spanish

2 tablespoons mixed fresh herbs, finely minced or 2 teaspoons crushed dried herbs

½ teaspoon salt or to taste

1 teaspoon caribe chile

Preheat the oven to 450 degrees F. Slice the potatoes lengthwise, then cut into ¾-inch-wide wedges. Place on a baking sheet and drizzle with the oil. Combine the herbs and chile, and using your hands, toss the seasoning to combine well with the potatoes.

Bake for 15 to 20 minutes (stirring after about 7 minutes for even baking), until the potatoes are tender and somewhat browned on the tips.

Variation: Sweet potatoes can be substituted.

Cooking Time: 15 to 20 minutes, Yield: 4 servings

PER SERVING:
Calories 163
Protein 3 g
Carbohydrates 31 g
Fiber 3 g
Fat 4 g
Saturated Fat 0 g
Cholesterol 0 mg
Sodium 10 mg

Sweet Potatoes with Chile and Herbs

Spice is extra nice on sweet potatoes and coupled with the balsamic vinegar and fresh herbs, it is very good. Cut in rounds, the potatoes are done in about 15 minutes and are just plain yummy with any poultry or pork dish.

2 medium to large sweet potatoes (about 1 pound)
2 tablespoons balsamic vinegar
1 tablespoon Basic Rub (page 176)
1 tablespoon fresh herbs, minced (such as sage or thyme) or 1 teaspoon ground dried herbs

Preheat the grill, or preheat the oven to 450 degrees F. Scrub the potatoes but leave unpeeled. Slice in ½-inch rounds.

Place the rounds on a baking sheet and sprinkle with the vinegar, followed by the rub and herbs. Bake for 15 to 20 minutes, until the potatoes are fork-tender. Serve hot.

Cooking Time: 15 to 20 minutes, Yield: 4 servings

PER SERVING:
Calories 81
Protein 1 g
Carbohydrates 19 g
Fiber 2 g
Fat 0 g
Saturated Fat 0 g
Cholesterol 0 mg
Sodium 513 mg

Salsa Verde Rice

The depth of flavor the Tomatillo Salsa brings to the rice
makes it very good as either a side dish or a light main dish—
especially if some beans or chunks of chicken breast are added.
Use vegetable broth, omit the chicken, and it becomes a very
good vegetarian dish.

2 cups chicken or vegetable broth

1 cup uncooked long-grain rice

About 1 teaspoon salt, if needed

1 cup Tomatillo Salsa (page 170)

1 clove garlic, minced

Cilantro leaves, for garnish (optional)

Bring the broth to a boil in a 3-quart saucepan with a close-fitting cover.
Add the rice. Taste to determine the need for salt.

Reduce the heat, cover, and simmer for 15 minutes or until all the liquid
is absorbed. Stir in the salsa and garlic. Taste and adjust the seasonings.
Garnish each serving with a cilantro leaf, if desired.

Cooking Time: 15 to 20 minutes, Yield: 4 servings

PER SERVING:
Calories 212
Protein 6 g
Carbohydrates 44 g
Fiber 2 g
Fat 2 g
Saturated Fat 1 g
Cholesterol 3 mg
Sodium 58 mg

Green Chile Cheese Rice

Green chile and cheese are totally meant for each other. This dish is so flavorful and is wonderful with most any entrée. Any kind of cheese can be used, and if calories or fat grams need to be reduced, use less cheese of a highly-flavored type such as extra sharp Cheddar. 🌶

2 cups chicken or vegetable broth or stock

1 cup uncooked long-grain rice

About 1 teaspoon of salt, if needed

½ cup green chiles, parched, peeled, and chopped or 1 4-ounce can

½ cup grated Cheddar cheese or mixed Monterey and Cheddar, or more to taste

½ cup nonfat sour cream, or to taste

Bring the stock to a boil in a 3-quart saucepan with a close-fitting cover. Add the rice. Reduce the heat, cover, and simmer for 15 minutes, or until the rice is soft and fluffy and all the liquid is absorbed. Remove from the heat and stir in the chiles, cheese, and sour cream. Cover for 3 to 5 minutes for the cheese to melt and the flavors to blend. Taste and adjust seasoning. Add more cheese, if desired. Serve hot.

Cooking Time: 15 to 20 minutes, Yield: 4 servings

PER SERVING:
Calories 287
Protein 11 g
Carbohydrates 49 g
Fiber 1 g
Fat 6 g
Saturated Fat 4 g
Cholesterol 20 mg
Sodium 170 mg
(Analyzed with Cheddar cheese.)

Snappy Beans and Rice

Sometimes called Hopping John in the South, this combination has long been a favorite when supermarkets had "lean pickings." It is honestly a meal in itself, especially when so flavorful with the chile. ♪

2 cups cooked rice

1 16-ounce can pinto or black beans, drained (2 cups cooked)

½ cup green chiles, parched, peeled, and chopped or 1 4-ounce can

1 teaspoon ground pure hot red chile, or more to suit taste

1 teaspoon freshly ground cumin, or more to suit taste

Broth (any kind), if needed

In a large bowl, combine the rice, beans, chopped chiles, ground chile, and cumin. After tasting, determine the need for more chile and cumin and add to suit taste. Cover with plastic wrap and microwave on high for 2 minutes (see Note). Stir, taste, and adjust the seasonings. Serve hot.

Note: To cook rice, follow the package instructions, or for 2 cups cooked rice, bring 1 ½ cups water to boil with ½ teaspoon salt in a 3-quart saucepan with a close-fitting cover. When boiling, add ⅔ cup regular long- or medium-grain rice. Stir and reduce heat, then cover when it comes to a simmer. Cook for 15 minutes without removing the cover. Check for doneness and fluff with a fork.

To cook this meal conventionally: In a heavy, 3-quart saucepan, combine ¼ cup water or broth (any kind), the rice, beans, chopped chiles, ground chile, and cumin. Stir and cook, uncovered, for 3 to 5 minutes on medium-low heat.

Cooking Time: 2 to 5 minutes, Yield: 4 servings

PER SERVING:
Calories 243
Protein 10 g
Carbohydrates 49 g
Fiber 9 g
Fat 2 g
Saturated Fat 0 g
Cholesterol 0 mg
Sodium 245 mg

Very Quick Refritos

The secret to flavorful refried beans is "tingeing" the garlic, or sautéing it until it just begins to turn tan. Even canned beans come to life with toasted garlic. ʒ

2 teaspoons unsalted butter, bacon drippings, or lard
2 cloves garlic, minced
1 16-ounce can refried beans or whole pinto beans without fat
1 teaspoon pickled jalapeños, chopped, or to suit taste

In a heavy, seasoned skillet over medium-high heat, melt the butter. Add the garlic, stirring constantly. When the garlic begins to turn tan, add the beans. Stir if refried; mash with a masher if whole. If the beans become dry, add broth or water. Stir in the jalapeños. Serve hot to accompany a southwestern meal, or use as an ingredient in other dishes.

Cooking Time: 6 to 8 minutes for refried beans, 12 to 15 minutes for whole beans, Yield: 4 servings

PER SERVING:
Calories 126
Protein 6 g
Carbohydrates 18 g
Fiber 6 g
Fat 3 g
Saturated Fat 2 g
Cholesterol 14 mg
Sodium 359 mg
(Analyzed with butter.)

Chilied Cheesy Grits

Grits are totally Southern, yet they are popular in Texas, which is dead center between the Deep South and the West. Grits became popular in the West because so many Southerners kept moving farther and farther west, and they took their grits with them. These are good as a side dish with most any meat or with eggs for breakfast.

You can also use the grits as a base for seared vegetables. Just slice the seared vegetables into thin strips and serve over the hot grits. You may wish to omit the cheese from the grits when serving them this way. ❦

½ cup quick-cooking grits

2 cloves garlic, minced

½ cup green chiles, parched, peeled, and chopped or 1 4-ounce can

½ cup grated Cheddar cheese, preferably low fat

Bring 2 cups water to a boil, then slowly add the grits, stirring constantly. Reduce the heat to low, cover, and cook for 5 to 7 minutes, until all the water is absorbed.

Add the garlic, chiles, and cheese. Cook, stirring, for about 2 minutes, or until the cheese melts. Serve immediately.

Variations: Make red chile grits by substituting 2 tablespoons ground pure red chiles for the green chiles. Stir in the chiles until the grits are uniformly pinkish red.

Cooking Time: 5 to 7 minutes, Yield: 4 servings

PER SERVING:
Calories 111
Protein 6 g
Carbohydrates 19 g
Fiber 1 g
Saturated Fat 1 g
Cholesterol 3 mg
Sodium 88 mg
(Analyzed with low-fat
Cheddar cheese.)

Spicy Sesame Spinach

Spinach is one of our mainstays. It is high in nutrition and yet low in calories. I can remember to this day my ecstasy when I learned that there were only 8 calories in each cup of fresh spinach, which I had hated as a child. If you want, you may cook kale this same way. Kale is the most healthful of all greens. Or you can add kale to this dish for added nutrition. Just steam the Kale first after the seeds are toasted for about 5 minutes, then add the spinach. The flavors are great. As a variation, I sometimes drizzle a little cold pressed extra-virgin olive oil over the greens when done for added flavor. 🌿

1 tablespoon sesame seeds

3 cups fresh spinach, loosely packed and well-rinsed

1 ½ teaspoons red wine vinegar, or to taste

½ teaspoon crushed red pequin quebrado flakes, or to taste

In a heavy skillet over medium heat, toast the sesame seeds for 2 to 3 minutes, stirring frequently.

Add the spinach, cover, reduce heat to low, and cook for about 5 minutes, or until wilted. Season with vinegar and chile, adding more if desired, and serve.

Cooking Time: 6 to 7 minutes, Yield: 2 servings

PER SERVING:
Calories 204
Protein 4 g
Carbohydrates 42 g
Fiber 4 g
Fat 2 g
Saturated Fat 1 g
Cholesterol 6 mg
Sodium 241 mg
(Analyzed with skim milk.)

Orange Caribe Steamed Cabbage

Cabbage tends to be a forgotten vegetable for serving cooked. The orange, sesame oil, and pequin chile make this a very flavorful side dish for most any fish or meat main meal. We had it first with salmon, and it was wonderful.

1 tablespoon vegetable oil

4 cups cabbage, finely shredded (½ head)

About ½ teaspoon salt

Few grinds of black pepper

Zest of 1 orange, chopped

1 teaspoon sesame oil, or to taste

½ teaspoon pequin quebrado, or to taste

2 tablespoons freshly squeezed orange juice

Warm the vegetable oil in a sauté pan over medium-high heat. Add the cabbage and sprinkle with the salt and pepper. Toss and cook, stirring, for 3 to 5 minutes, until the cabbage is slightly wilted.

Add the zest, pequin, sesame oil, and juice; cook for another 2 to 3 minutes. Taste and adjust the seasonings. Serve immediately.

Preparation Time: 5 to 7 minutes, Yield: 4 servings

PER SERVING:
Calories 62
Protein 1 g
Carbohydrates 5 g
Fiber 2 g
Fat 5 g
Saturated Fat 1 g
Cholesterol 0 mg
Sodium 303 mg

Stove-Top Grilled Veggies

Grilling brings out the natural flavors in vegetables and is a wonderful way to make them appealing. You can vary the vegetables according to what you have on hand and to complement the other foods you are serving.

1 eggplant

1 teaspoon salt, or to taste

8 scallions or 1 medium onion, sliced ¼ inch thick

1 red bell pepper, cut into ½-inch-wide strips

2 small zucchini, sliced into ¼-inch-thick strips

Dressing (recipe follows)

DRESSING

2 tablespoons extra-virgin olive oil, preferably Spanish

Juice of 1 lime

2 cloves garlic, minced

1 teaspoon ground pure hot red chile (optional)

About 30 minutes before you plan to cook the vegetables, prepare the eggplant. (You can also prepare it hours ahead or even up to 15 minutes ahead.) Using a meat fork, cut through the skin of the eggplant to a depth of about ⅛ inch. Slice into rounds a scant ½ inch thick. Lightly salt each side of each slice, then place the slices on a plate, with a double layer of paper toweling between each layer of slices.

Place wood chips or dried herb stalks in the water pan of a stove-top grill. Add water, following the manufacturer's instructions, then preheat the grill to medium.

Pat both sides of the eggplant slices dry. Place on the grill, then add the scallions, bell pepper, and zucchini as there is room. Grill the vegetables for 3 to 4 minutes per side. Remove to a platter, keeping the vegetables of each kind together.

Prepare the Dressing. Uniformly sprinkle it over the vegetables and serve.

TO MAKE THE DRESSING: Combine the oil, lime juice, garlic, and chile, if using. Variation: Toss the grilled vegetables together and serve over Chilied Cheesy Grits (page 155).

Cooking Time: 5 to 8 minutes, Yield: 4 servings

PER SERVING:
Calories 118
Protein 2 g
Carbohydrates 13 g
Fiber 4 g
Fat 7 g
Saturated Fat 1 g
Cholesterol 0 mg
Sodium 588 mg
(Analyzed with 1 teaspoon salt for the eggplant and 1 medium onion instead of scallions.)

Mexican Style Grilled Corn

Grilling corn really sets the flavor apart. The grilling heightens the flavor. Using really fresh corn is a must, and take care to not over grill. Just cook until it gets little dark brown flecks on some of the kernels. Grilled corn is a street snack in much of Mexico and is served with hot, spicy mayonnaise. Try it; you will be amazed at how good it is.

4 large ears fresh, sweet corn

2 teaspoons vegetable or olive oil

Preheat the cooking surface. Husk the corn and remove the silk. Lightly oil each ear, then place on the grill and cook until the kernels, when pierced, are firm and not milky. The outside edges of the kernels should be a bit blackened.

Cooking Time: 5 to 6 minutes, Yield: 4 servings

Serve with your choice of the following toppings:

FRESH LIME AND CARIBE CHILE:

1 lime, cut into wedges

4 teaspoons crushed red caribe chile

Serve lime wedges—2 per person, per ear—along with a small bowl of chile

NEW MEXICAN HERBS

2 tablespoons extra-virgin olive oil

½ teaspoon ground Mexican oregano

½ teaspoon ground cumin

½ teaspoon crushed pequin quebrado chiles

Before grilling the corn, combine the oil, oregano, cumin, and chiles. Serve with the hot corn.

MEXICAN HOT MAYONNAISE

4 tablespoons (¼ cup) mayonnaise

1 small jalapeño, minced

Combine the mayonnaise and jalapeño. Serve with the hot corn

PER SERVING:
(Corn)
Calories 8
Protein 0 g
Carbohydrates 2 g
Fiber 1 g
Fat 0 g
Saturated Fat 0 g
Cholesterol 0 mg
Sodium 0 mg

PER SERVING:
(Lime topping)
Calories 8
Protein 0 g
Carbohydrates 2 g
Fiber 1 g
Fat 0 g
Saturated Fat 0 g
Cholesterol 0 mg
Sodium 0 mg

PER SERVING:
(Herb topping)
Calories 62
Protein 0 g
Carbohydrates 0 g
Fiber 0 g
Fat 7 g
Saturated Fat 1 g
Cholesterol 0 mg
Sodium 1 mg

PER SERVING:
(Mayonnaise topping)
Calories 103
Protein 0 g
Carbohydrates 1 g
Fiber 0 g
Fat 11 g
Saturated Fat 2 g
Cholesterol 10 mg
Sodium 76 mg

Spicy Broccoli Sauté

Broccoli is one of those vegetables that is often touted as being very good for you, yet so many do not like it because it is boringly prepared—cooked to death and served plain. Even diehard broccoli haters will be tempted with this recipe, if you can just get them to taste it! 🌶

2 large heads broccoli

2 tablespoons olive oil, preferably Spanish

3 cloves garlic

2 tablespoons crushed caribe chile

Wash the broccoli and cut the florets no more than ½ inch thick. Meanwhile, warm the oil in a seasoned, deep skillet over medium-high heat. Stir in the garlic and immediately add the broccoli.

Cook for about 3 minutes, or until the florets are somewhat browned on the edges. Sir to turn over the florets and cook to the desired doneness. Remove from the heat and add the chile. Stir, then remove to a serving bowl or to the plates. Serve immediately.

Cooking Time: 5 to 8 minutes, Yield: 4 servings

PER SERVING:
Calories 98
Protein 3 g
Carbohydrates 7 g
Fiber 4 g
Fat 7 g
Saturated Fat 1 g
Cholesterol 0 mg
Sodium 29 mg

Quick Corn Custard with Chiles

You may have noticed how often green chiles are paired with corn. It is because they are so compatible. This is a marvelous side dish, good enough for the finest company and quick and easy to prepare. It is very good in winter, as it is best with the canned cream-style corn. ♪

1 15 ½-ounce can cream-style corn

1 teaspoon unsalted butter

1 egg, beaten

2 corn tortillas, torn into small pieces

½ cup green chiles, parched, peeled, and chopped or 1 4-ounce can

Preheat the oven to 375 degrees F. Butter 4 6-ounce ramekins or 6 4-ounce ramekins. In a blender or food processor, combine the corn, butter, egg, and tortillas. Process until puréed.

Stir in the chiles but do not process. Pour the mixture into the ramekins and place them on a baking sheet. Bake for 15 to 20 minutes, until an inserted knife comes out clean. Serve at once.

Cooking Time: 15 minutes, Yield: 4 to 6 servings

PER SERVING:
(1/6 recipe)
Calories 96
Protein 3 g
Carbohydrates 19 g
Fiber 2 g
Fat 2 g
Saturated Fat 1 g
Cholesterol 37 mg
Sodium 24 mg

Sauces & Salsas

Having a well-stocked pantry and freezer
with the following condiments can greatly
trim the preparation time for any of the recipes.
Whenever you are making any of the following
recipes, go ahead and double or quadruple the
recipe and freeze in quantities you will most often use.
Freezing in the smallest amounts is best for most convenience—you can always use more than one container.
Sauces, especially salsas, are the personality of
Southwest cuisine. They provide accent and flavor,
are nutritious, and low in fat. I have also included
in this chapter some other spicy condiments that
are nice to have around, such as a Basic Rub on
page 176 and Hot Honey on page 177.

Basic Red Chile Sauce

This is my favorite red chile sauce, which is the basis for enchiladas and for saucing over chiles rellenos, tamales, and traditional southwestern specialties. You'll notice that I make my red sauce from chile powder. High-quality, ground pure chile powders are so much faster, consistent, and nutritious than whole pods.

1 tablespoon unsalted butter or lard
2 tablespoons all-purpose flour
¼ cup ground pure mild red New Mexican chile powder
2 cups broth (beef, chicken, or vegetable)
1 clove garlic, minced
Pinch each of ground or dried Mexican oregano and freshly ground cumin
Salt (optional)

In a heavy saucepan, melt the butter. Add the flour and cook, stirring, until the mixture turns slightly golden. Remove the pan from the cooking heat and stir in the chile powders. Stir in the stock. Continue stirring until the mixture becomes smooth.

Add the garlic, oregano, and cumin and simmer for about 10 minutes. Taste and adjust the seasonings, adding salt, if desired.

Variation: Ground chuck, roast beef, pork, or poached chicken or turkey can be added when making enchiladas.

Preparation Time: about 15 minutes, Yield: 2 cups, or 4 servings

PER SERVING:
Calories 90
Protein 3 g
Carbohydrates 12 g
Fiber 4 g
Fat 4 g
Saturated Fat 2 g
Cholesterol 8 mg
Sodium 363 mg
(Analyzed with butter.)

Favorite Green Chile Sauce

This is the all-time best green chile sauce. It beats the thickened chile juice sauces and the tomato-based ones, hands down. You can add chunks of poached chicken or seafood to the sauce for fabulous enchiladas. It is a favorite sauce for burritos, chimichangas and other southwestern entrees.

1 tablespoon unsalted butter or lard

½ cup onion, chopped

2 tablespoons all-purpose flour

1 ½ cups chicken or vegetable broth

1 cup green chiles, parched and chopped, or 2 4-ounce cans, drained

1 large clove garlic, finely minced

Salt (optional)

In a heavy saucepan, melt the butter. Add the onion and sauté until it is clear. Add the flour, gradually stir in the broth, and cook until the mixture is smooth. Add the chiles and garlic and simmer for 10 minutes. Taste and adjust the seasonings, adding salt, if desired.

Cooking Time: about 15 minutes, Yield: about 2 cups, or 4 servings

PER SERVING:
Calories 71
Protein 3 g
Carbohydrates 8 g
Fiber 1 g
Fat 4 g
Saturated Fat 2 g
Cholesterol 10 mg
Sodium 74 mg

Hotter-Than-Fire Dressing

¾ cup spicy hot tomato juice (approximately 1 5 ½-ounce can)

3 tablespoons cider vinegar

1 fresh jalapeño, minced

1 teaspoon ground red pequin quebrado chile

2 cloves garlic, minced

2 tablespoons extra-virgin olive oil, preferably Spanish

PER SERVING:
(2 tablespoons)
Calories 38
Protein 0 g
Carbohydrates 2 g
Fiber 0 g
Fat 3 g
Saturated Fat 0 g
Cholesterol 0 mg
Sodium 83 mg

Combine the tomato juice, vinegar, jalapeño, pequin chile, garlic, and oil. Whisk together, or place in a jar and shake.

Preparation Time: 5 minutes, Yield 1 cup

Hot Red Chile Dressing

This dressing has a wine base rather than the spicy tomato one used in the Hotter-Than-Fire Dressing. It will keep at least a month in the refrigerator.

¼ cup dry white wine

2 large cloves garlic, minced

1 tablespoon Dijon mustard

1 teaspoon hot red chile

2 tablespoons red wine or balsamic vinegar

1 tablespoon extra-virgin olive oil, preferably Spanish

PER SERVING:
(1/4 recipe)
Calories 47
Protein 0 g
Carbohydrates 1 g
Fiber 0 g
Fat 4 g
Saturated Fat 0 g
Cholesterol 0 mg
Sodium 97 mg

Combine the wine, garlic, mustard, red chile, vinegar, and oil. Whisk together, or place in a jar and shake.

Preparation Time: 5 minutes, Yield: ½ cup (enough for 1 4-serving salad)

Jalapeño Lime Cream Dressing

1 cup plain yoghurt or ¾ cup nonfat sour cream
with ¼ cup skim milk whisked in
1 or 2 jalapeños, minced
¼ cup cilantro, coarsely chopped
2 teaspoons freshly squeezed lime juice (½ lime)
½ teaspoon lime zest

Combine the yoghurt, jalapeños, cilantro, lime juice, and zest. Whisk together, or place in a jar and shake. This dressing will keep at least 2 weeks covered in the refrigerator.

Preparation Time: 5 minutes, Yield: 1 cup

PER SERVING:
(2 tablespoons)
Calories 20
Protein 2 g
Carbohydrates 3 g
Fiber 0 g
Fat 0 g
Saturated Fat 0 g
Cholesterol 1 mg
Sodium 24 mg

Spicy Cilantro Lime Dressing

3 tablespoons freshly squeezed lime juice (1 or 2 limes)
1 tablespoon honey, preferably desert blossom
1 tablespoon cilantro, coarsely chopped
½ jalapeño, minced
Pinch of salt (optional)

Combine the lime juice, honey, cilantro, and jalapeño. Whisk until well blended. Taste and adjust the seasonings, adding salt, if needed.

Preparation Time: 5 minutes, Yield: ½ cup (enough for 1 4-serving salad)

PER SERVING:
(1/4 recipe)
Calories 21
Protein 0 g
Carbohydrates 6 g
Fiber 0 g
Fat 0 g
Saturated Fat 0 g
Cholesterol 0 mg
Sodium 1 mg

Creamy Ranch-Style Dressing

A healthier, spicy version of the original.

¾ cup plain nonfat yoghurt

¼ cup low-fat mayonnaise

1 tablespoon cider vinegar or white vinegar

1 tablespoon Dijon mustard

2 teaspoons fresh thyme, minced or 1 teaspoon dried, crushed

1 scallion, white and tender green parts, minced

1 jalapeño, minced

In a small bowl, combine the yoghurt, mayonnaise, vinegar, mustard, thyme, scallion, and jalapeño. Whisk together to combine well. Refrigerate for an hour or more before serving.

Preparation time: 5 minutes, Yield: 1 cup

PER SERVING:
(2 tablespoons)
Calories 41
Protein 2 g
Carbohydrates 3 g
Fiber 0 g
Fat 3 g
Saturated Fat 1 g
Cholesterol 0 mg
Sodium 120 mg

Hot New Mexican Table Salsa

This salsa is the darling of the restaurant industry because it keeps so well, is easy to make, and can be frozen. It is sometimes called Salsa Rojo or Salsa Colorado. Coarsely minced cilantro can be folded in, if desired.

1 14 ½-ounce can peeled tomatoes (without added herbs or seasonings), diced

2 teaspoons finely crushed red pequin chile, or to taste

1 ½ teaspoons ground cumin

2 cloves garlic, minced

Combine the tomatoes, chile, vinegar, cumin, and garlic. Allow to stand for at least 10 minutes before serving.

Variations: Substitute 1 tablespoon freshly squeezed lime juice for 1 tablespoon of the cider vinegar. Add a generous pinch of chopped fresh Mexican oregano and some coarsely chopped cilantro, if desired.

Preparation Time: 5 minutes, Yield: 1 ¾ cup, or 3 to 6 servings

PER SERVING:
(1/6 recipe)
Calories 28
Protein 1 g
Carbohydrates 6 g
Fiber 2 g
Fat 0 g
Saturated Fat 0 g
Cholesterol 0 mg
Sodium 92 mg

Salsa Fresca

This original salsa, commemorating the Mexican flag, was made with equal parts of red, green, and white: red tomatoes, green chiles, and white onions. This versatile salsa is about as good as it gets for most everything—as a dipping salsa, over meats of any kind, or on traditional dishes such as tacos and burritos. Should any ever be left over, make it into a vinaigrette salad dressing or freeze it for use in chile con queso or as a sauce for huevos rancheros.

1 cup red, ripe tomato, chopped into ½-inch dice

1 cup white Spanish onion, chopped into ¼-inch dice

1 cup green chiles, parched, peeled, and diced, or 2 4-ounce cans, drained

1 clove garlic, minced

½ cup cilantro, coarsely chopped

Salt (optional)

Combine the tomato, onion, chiles, garlic, and cilantro. Allow to stand for about 10 minutes before serving. Taste and add salt, if desired.

Preparation Time: 10 minutes, Yield: 3 cups, or 4 to 6 servings

PER SERVING:
(1/6 recipe)
Calories 27
Protein 1 g
Carbohydrates 6 g
Fiber 1 g
Fat 0 g
Saturated Fat 0 g
Cholesterol 0 mg
Sodium 6 mg

Tomatillo Salsa (Mexican Salsa Verde)

The fruity, fresh flavor of this salsa when made with fresh or frozen tomatillos is the best—far better than the canned variety. A variation is to sear the cut side of the halved tomatillos in a heavy, seasoned skillet until browned on the cut side. Turn the tomatillos over, remove from the heat, place a close-fitting lid on top and steam until soft. Do this instead of boiling the tomatillos. The flavor is more intense and rich, however the color is more brownish and not so pretty as the fresh spring-green color of the boiled tomatillos. ρ

About 8 ounces fresh tomatillos (1 ½ cups husked)

1 fresh jalapeño

1 1-inch wedge fresh onion (about ¼ cup)

¼ cup fresh cilantro leaves (including tops of stalks)

Salt

Pour about an inch of water into a saucepan with a lid and bring to a boil. Meanwhile, husk the tomatillos, rinse, and cut the larger ones to be the same size as the others for even cooking. Cook the tomatillos for 5 to 7 minutes, until fork-tender. Drain, reserving some of the liquid. Place the tomatillos, jalapeño, onion, and cilantro in a blender or food processor and process until puréed, adding reserved juice as desired for consistency.

Preparation Time: 15 minutes, Yield: About 1 ½ cups, or 4 servings

PER SERVING:
Calories 23
Protein 1 g
Carbohydrates 4 mg
Fiber 1 g
Fat 1 g
Saturated Fat 0 g
Cholesterol 0 mg
Sodium 2 mg

Cucumber Salsa

This crunchy salsa is great over seafood of any kind. 🌶

1 medium cucumber, scored with a fork and thinly sliced (see Note)
1 medium sweet white onion, finely diced
1 tablespoon freshly squeezed lime juice (about ½ lime)
1 teaspoon crushed red caribe chile

In a medium bowl, combine the cucumber, onion, lime juice, and chile;
toss together. Allow to marinate for a few minutes before serving.

Note: To score a cucumber with a fork, hold the tines firmly
against the skin and pull the fork along the length of the cucumber.
Repeat until the entire outside of the cucumber is scored.

Preparation Time: about 5 minutes, Yield: about 2 cups, or 4 servings

PER SERVING:
Calories 24
Protein 1 g
Carbohydrates 5 g
Fiber 1 g
Fat 0 g
Saturated Fat 0 g
Cholesterol 0 mg
Sodium 2 mg

Chipotle Cantaloupe Salsa

This salsa could be used as a dipping salsa with vegetables or chips.
The smoky chipotle stands up to the perfumey cantaloupe. 🌶

1 dried chipotle chile, reconstituted and finely chopped
1 medium red onion, diced
½ cantaloupe, peeled and cut into ½-inch cubes
1 tablespoon freshly squeezed lime juice (about ½ lime)
2 tablespoons cilantro, coarsely chopped

In a medium bowl, combine the chipotle, onion, cantaloupe, lime juice,
and cilantro; stir together. Taste; if desired, add some of the stewing
liquid from the chipotles.

Preparation Time: 5 to 7 minutes, Yield: About 2 cups, or 4 servings

PER SERVING:
Calories 36
Protein 1 g
Carbohydrates 9 g
Fiber 1 g
Fat 0 g
Saturated Fat 0 g
Cholesterol 0 mg
Sodium 7 mg

Mango Salsa

Mangoes are one of my favorite fruits. To me, they taste like a gingered peach. The fruity flavor is complemented nicely with spicy pequin, making it a terrific salsa for any seafood or poultry dish. I have even served it with jicama sticks and corn chips for snacking or as an appetizer. 〗

¾ cup mango, chopped into ½-inch cubes
¾ cup Spanish onion, diced
¼ cup cilantro, coarsely chopped
2 tablespoons balsamic vinegar
1 tablespoon crushed red pequin quebrado

PER SERVING:
Calories 41
Protein 1 g
Carbohydrates 10 g
Fiber 2 g
Fat 0 g
Saturated Fat 0 g
Cholesterol 0 mg
Sodium 6 mg

Combine the mango, onion, cilantro, vinegar, and chile; toss together. Allow the flavors to blend for at least 10 to 15 minutes before serving.

Preparation Time: 5 to 7 minutes, Yield: 1 ½ cups, or 3 or 4 servings

Sweet Pear Pineapple Salsa

This sweet salsa combines the mellow flavor of pear with pineapple and the tart craisins or dried cranberries. The chile pulls all of the flavors together. Pork, poultry, or seafood are each equally good with this salsa. ⎰

1 Anjou or Bartlett pear, peeled, cored, and diced
1 8-ounce can crushed pineapple, drained
1 cup dried cranberries or craisins
½ teaspoon crushed red pequin quebrado, or more to taste

PER SERVING:
Calories 78
Protein 0 g
Carbohydrates 0 g
Fiber 2 g
Fat 0 g
Saturated Fat 0 g
Cholesterol 0 mg
Sodium 145 mg

In a nonreactive bowl, combine the pear, pineapple, cranberries, and chile. Allow to stand for at least 10 minutes before serving.

Preparation Time: 5 to 7 minutes, Yield: About 2 ½ cups, or 4 generous servings

Cilantro Salsa

Cilantro's fresh taste can tame the most fiery dish. This salsa pairs well with a main dish of almost any kind. 🌶

½ cup onion, chopped

1 cup red bell pepper, chopped

1 small jalapeño, minced

¼ cup cilantro, coarsely chopped

2 tablespoons lemon juice

In a nonreactive bowl, combine the onion, bell pepper, jalapeño, cilantro, and lemon juice. Allow to stand for at least 10 minutes before serving.

Preparation Time: 5 minutes, Yield: About 1 ¾ cup, or 4 servings

PER SERVING:
Calories 22
Protein 1 g
Carbohydrates 5 g
Fiber 1 g
Fat 0 g
Saturated Fat 0 g
Cholesterol 0 mg
Sodium 2 mg

White Bean Salsa

1 15-ounce can white beans, drained

2 cloves garlic, minced

4 scallions, tender green tops included, thinly sliced

2 tablespoons white wine vinegar

2 tablespoons extra-virgin olive oil, preferably Spanish

1 teaspoon pequin quebrado chile

¼ cup cilantro, coarsely chopped

Combine the beans, garlic, scallions, vinegar, oil, chile, and cilantro. Allow to stand for at least 10 minutes before serving.

Preparation Time: 5 minutes, Yield: 4 servings

PER SERVING:
Calories 191
Protein 9 g
Carbohydrates 24 g
Fiber g
Fat 7 g
Saturated Fat 1 g
Cholesterol 9 mg
Sodium 220 mg

Cilantro Pesto

This is a takeoff on the Italian favorite that is made with basil. Cilantro and chile paired together make for a sauce that is terrific in such dishes as the Chevre Wrap, page 137 or on most any kind of pasta. You can even tame it somewhat and add olive oil and vinegar in equal parts to make a zesty salad dressing for your favorite greens.

¼ cup extra-virgin olive oil
1 cup loosely packed cilantro leaves
2 tablespoons roasted piñons
2 large cloves garlic
1 fresh jalapeño
⅓ cup grated Romano or Parmesan cheese

In a blender combine the oil, cilantro, piñons, garlic, jalapeño, and cheese. Process until smooth.

Preparation Time: 3 to 5 minutes, Yield: 1 cup

PER SERVING:
(1/4 cup)
Calories 184
Protein 3 g
Carbohydrates 2 g
Fiber 1 g
Fat 18 g
Saturated Fat 4 g
Cholesterol 9 mg
Sodium 105 mg
(Analyzed with
Romano cheese.)

Pico de Gallo

This is the traditional fajita salsa. It should be made with chipotles; however, if unavailable, fresh jalapeños, minced, may be substituted. Other juicy fruits can be substituted for the tomatoes, such as nectarines, peaches, plums, strawberries, or watermelon.

2 dried chipotle chiles, reconstituted, plus about 2 tablespoons of the juice
1 cup red, ripe tomato, diced (1 large or 2 small)
1 cup onion, chopped (1 large)
2 cloves garlic, minced
¼ cup cilantro, coarsely chopped
Juice of 1 lime

Combine the chiles and juice, the tomato, onion, garlic, cilantro, and lime juice. Set aside for 5 to 10 minutes for the flavors to blend.

Preparation Time: 10 minutes, Yield: about 2 cups, or 4 servings

PER SERVING:
Calories 30
Protein 1 g
Carbohydrates 7 g
Fiber 1 g
Fat 0 g
Saturated Fat 0 g
Cholesterol 0 mg
Sodium 6 mg

Just Peachy Salsa

This salsa is great over veal chops, lamb, pork, or poultry. It is best when made with juicy, fresh peaches in season. It can also double as an appetizer.

2 large, ripe peaches, peeled and chopped
½ cup red onion, chopped
¼ cup crushed red caribe chile
2 tablespoons lemon juice
¼ cup flat-leaf parsley or cilantro, coarsely chopped

Combine the peaches, onion, chile, lemon juice, and parsley. Taste and adjust the seasonings. Allow to stand for at least 5 minutes before serving.

Preparation Time: 5 to 7 minutes, Yield: 4 servings

PER SERVING:
Calories 62
Protein 2 g
Carbohydrates 14 g
Fiber 4 g
Fat 1 g
Saturated Fat 0 g
Cholesterol 0 mg
Sodium 9 mg
(Analyzed with cilantro.)

Black-eyed Pea Salsa

This salsa is made with the good luck pea of the South and is great over pork chops, or over roast chicken.

2 cups cooked black-eyed peas (1 15-ounce can, drained)
½ cup white onion, chopped
2 cloves garlic, minced
⅓ cup pickled jalapeños, chopped

Combine the peas, onion, garlic, and jalapeños. Allow to stand for about 5 minutes before serving.

Preparation Time: 5 minutes, Yield: 4 servings

PER SERVING:
Calories 88
Protein 3 g
Carbohydrates 19 g
Fiber 5 g
Fat 0 g
Saturated Fat 0 g
Cholesterol 0 mg
Sodium 233 mg

Basic Rub

Rubs have long been popular in the Southwest for applying to meats before grilling or roasting. There are many variations; however, I think it is hard to improve on this basic recipe. You can alter the ingredients to please your palate. Make lots; it freezes well and is convenient to have on hand for quick meals. When using, place some of the rub in a shallow bowl and spoon it onto meat or vegetables. Then rub it in. Rub off any excess with a paper towel.

½ cup salt

½ cup freshly ground black pepper

½ cup ground pure mild red chile

2 tablespoons garlic granules

2 tablespoons sugar

Combine the salt, pepper, chile, garlic, and sugar in a jar. Freeze until ready to use.

Preparation Time: 3 to 5 minutes, Yield: 1 ¾ cups

PER SERVING:
(1 tablespoon)
Calories 15
Protein 1 g
Carbohydrates 3 g
Fiber 1 g
Fat 0 g
Saturated Fat 0 g
Cholesterol 0 mg
Sodium 1,996 mg
(Note: The salt supplies
100 percent of the sodium;
you can use a salt substitute.)

Hot Honey

I absolutely love this hot honey on hot buttered biscuits or corn-bread. It is great as a glaze for pork roast, chicken, and duck or as an ingredient in salad dressings or marinades.

2 tablespoons ground pure hot chile
1 cup desert blossom honey or any good-quality honey

In a 4-cup liquid measuring cup, combine the chiles and honey. Warm for about a minute in the microwave oven (see Note). Stir and allow to cool, then transfer to a jar and keep for later use.

Note: If you do not have a microwave oven, combine the ingredients in a jar and place in the sun for a week, or heat the mixture in a heavy saucepan over medium-low heat for 5 minutes.

Preparation Time: 3 minutes, Yield: 1 cup

PER SERVING:
(1 tablespoon)
Calories 67
Protein 0 g
Carbohydrates 18 g
Fiber 0 g
Fat 0 g
Saturated Fat 0 g
Cholesterol 0 mg
Sodium 10 mg

Desserts

These light, innovative desserts are takeoffs on more traditional desserts. Each can be made in twenty minutes or less. Many pair chiles with the ingredients—for extra fun and good health!

Calientes Manzanas

These are great fun to make. My daughter always loved them, and when she was a toddler, I called them Amy's Apples. For her, I left out the chile. They are striking to look at in a wine goblet and are particularly yummy with the frozen vanilla yoghurt. ✎

4 baking apples
4 ounces (½ cup) red-hot candies
2 teaspoons crushed red pequin quebrado chiles
Frozen yoghurt, vanilla or butter pecan (optional)

Wash the apples, then core, removing the entire seed sack. Combine the red hots and chiles; stuff into the middle of each apple. To microwave, place each apple in a wineglass (see Note).

Cover with plastic wrap and cook one at a time for 2 to 3 minutes. Serve as is or with a scoop of frozen yoghurt.

Note: Use a simple, everyday wine glass, not a carved or leaded glass, in the microwave.

To bake conventionally, stuff the apples and place them in a buttered baking pan. Bake, uncovered, at 375 degrees F. for 1 hour.

Cooking Time: 2 ½ to 3 minutes in a microwave oven, 1 hour in a conventional oven, Yield: 4 servings

PER SERVING:
(1 apple)
Calories 194
Protein 1 g
Carbohydrates 50 g
Fiber 4 g
Fat 1 g
Saturated Fat 0 g
Cholesterol 0 mg
Sodium 11 mg
(Analyzed with frozen yoghurt.)

Fruta Fresca Nachos

This dessert is similar to the Fruity Pizza, except here you cut the tortilla into pieces and toast them before constructing each. Select fruits of three different colors such as berries, peaches, and bananas or green grapes. You can either construct them or pass the fruit for each to construct their own.

4 flour tortillas (10-inch size)

2 tablespoons sugar

½ teaspoon ground cinnamon

2 cups mixed fruit cut into ½-inch dice

1 teaspoon pequin quebrado chile

1 3-ounce package nonfat cream cheese

1 to 2 tablespoons Triple Sec (optional)

Preheat the broiler. Slice each tortilla into 8 pie-shaped wedges. Combine the sugar and cinnamon in a shallow bowl. Quickly dip the tortilla wedges in water, drain briefly on paper toweling or a clean dishcloth, and dip one side in the cinnamon sugar. Arrange on a baking sheet without overlapping. Broil for 2 to 3 minutes, until toasted; let cool.

Place the fruit in a serving bowl, add chile, and stir well to combine. In another serving bowl, combine the cheese with the Triple Sec, if using.

Serve a plate of the cinnamon crisps and the bowls of fruit salsa and cheese, or, just before serving, spread the cheese on each cinnamon crisp and top with the salsa.

Preparation Time: About 15 minutes, Yield: 4 servings

PER SERVING:
Calories 315
Protein 10 g
Carbohydrates 56 g
Fiber 4 g
Fat 6 g
Saturated Fat 1 g
Cholesterol 2 mg
Sodium 462 mg
(Analyzed with watermelon, strawberries, and grapes.)

Fruity Tortilla Pizza

These are amazingly simple and they look elegant. The tortilla becomes the crust. Artfully arrange the fruit in a circular fashion as detailed below for a very pretty dessert.

1 flour tortilla (12-inch size)

1 cup grated Monterey Jack cheese, or ½ cup each cream cheese and grated Monterey Jack (see Note)

1 cup fresh strawberries, or 2 peaches or nectarines, peeled, pitted, and sliced

½ cup white seedless grapes or 2 or 3 kiwis, peeled

2 tablespoons fragrant honey

1 teaspoon caribe chile

Several shakes of ground cinnamon (optional)

Preheat the oven to 425 degrees F. Place the tortilla on a baking sheet and sprinkle with about two-thirds of the grated cheese.

Rinse the berries and pat dry. Remove the green stem and any bad spots. Arrange them, pointed tips up, in a circle about 1 inch in from the edge of the tortilla. Halve the grapes or slice the kiwis. Arrange in circles in the center.

Drizzle with honey, then sprinkle with the remaining cheese and the chile. If desired, shake cinnamon over all. Bake for 5 minutes, or until the cheese melts. Serve warm.

Note: If using a combination of cheeses, spread the cream cheese on the tortilla and sprinkle the Jack cheese over the fruit.

Cooking Time: 5 minutes, Yield: 4 servings

PER SERVING:
Calories 209
Protein 9 g
Carbohydrates 23 g
Fiber 2 g
Fat 10 g
Saturated Fat 6 g
Cholesterol 25 mg
Sodium 220 mg

Berry Blast

The berry flavor blasts right through the crispy topping. It is quite colorful, and pretty enough for company. You can vary the berries to suit the season—or use frozen if fresh are not available.

4 cups assorted fresh berries, such as strawberries, raspberries,
blueberries, and blackberries

1 lime

¼ cup sugar or honey

¾ cup each all-purpose flour and wheat flake cereal, crushed

2 tablespoons unsalted butter

1 teaspoon pequin chile

½ teaspoon ground cinnamon

½ cup apple juice concentrate

Frozen yoghurt or low-fat ice cream

Preheat the oven to 425 degrees F. Rinse the berries and place in a buttered baking dish. Squeeze the lime evenly over the top. Sprinkle with sugar. Combine the flour, cereal, butter, pequin chile, and cinnamon. Stir in the apple juice. Spread the batter over the berries. Bake for 15 to 20 minutes, until the topping is browned and crusty. Serve with frozen yoghurt or ice cream.

Baking Time: 15 to 20 minutes, Yield: 4 servings

PER SERVING:
Calories 339
Protein 5 g
Carbohydrates 68 g
Fiber 8 g
Fat 7 g
Saturated Fat 4 g
Cholesterol 16 mg
Sodium 63 mg

Spicy Broiled Pineapple

Pineapple takes well to grilling. The firm texture and sweet taste are accented by the hot chiles and sweet honey.

1 small, ripe pineapple or 1 14 ½-ounce can pineapple rings

3 tablespoons dark, flavorful, blossom honey or Hot Honey (page 177)

½ teaspoon, or to taste, ground hot red chile such as pequin or cayenne

2 tablespoons dark rum

If the grill is not already hot, preheat the broiler to high or use a microwave oven. To prepare the pineapple, hold it upright and slice vertically through the green top and down through the fruit, leaving the top attached to the pineapple. Cut the pineapple into quarters by slicing each half through the top. Cut off the rind.

Place each quarter pineapple, cut side up, in a microwavable baking dish (see Note). Mix the honey and chile and spread on the pineapple. Drizzle with the rum. Cook in the microwave oven on full power for 4 to 6 minutes, until hot.

Serve with the green top still attached. Spoon more of the honey mixture over the top.

Note: If grilling the pineapple, place each quarter on a baking sheet, drizzle with the honey mixture and rum, then transfer to the grill. If broiling, leave the pineapple on the baking sheet and broil for 5 to 8 minutes, until browned on the edges and hot throughout.

Cooking Time: 4 to 6 minutes in a microwave oven, 5 to 8 minutes under the broiler or on the grill, Yield: 4 servings

PER SERVING:
Calories 122
Protein 1 g
Carbohydrates 28 g
Fiber 2 g
Fat 1 g
Saturated Fat 0 g
Cholesterol 0 mg
Sodium 2 mg

Banana Oatmeal Cookies

These moist cookies spice up well. Do remember, they need to be kept in a tightly closed container and should be refrigerated or frozen if keeping longer than five days. 🌶

Nonstick oil spray
¾ cup mashed banana (3 small bananas)
¼ cup vegetable oil
1 12-ounce can apple juice concentrate
2 teaspoons vanilla extract
3 cups whole wheat or all-purpose flour
1 ¼ cups oatmeal, any kind
1 teaspoon ground hot chile
1 teaspoon baking soda

Preheat the oven to 375 degrees F. Spray 2 baking sheets with nonstick oil spray; set aside. In a mixing bowl or food processor, combine the banana, oil, juice, and vanilla.

In another bowl, combine the flour, oatmeal, chile, and baking soda. Add to the banana mixture and combine until well blended.

Drop by spoonsful onto the prepared baking sheets, leaving about 2 inches between each. Bake for 10 to 12 minutes, until firm when pressed with a finger. Transfer to cooling racks.

Baking Time: 10 to 12 minutes, Yield: 36 cookies

PER SERVING:
(1 cookie)
Calories 82
Protein 2 g
Carbohydrates 15 g
Fiber 2 g
Fat 2 g
Saturated Fat 0 g
Cholesterol 0 mg
Sodium 39 mg

Spicy Hot Chocolate Mousse

This mousse has a fabulous flavor even with the lack of the usual heavy cream. Do use the best quality chocolate you can lay your hands on, as that will go a long way toward setting the velvety richness.

½ cup sugar, divided

4 ounces (4 squares) high-quality bittersweet baking chocolate

2 tablespoons unsalted butter, cut into small bits

1 tablespoon red-hot schnapps

3 egg whites

1 teaspoon caribe chile

In a liquid measuring cup, combine ¼ cup water and ¼ cup of the sugar. Microwave for 1 minute on full power to dissolve the sugar, or, on a conventional range, bring to a boil in a small saucepan and cook until dissolved. Set aside.

In a heavy saucepan or a double boiler over medium-low heat, combine the chocolate and butter, whisking continuously until melted and of a creamy texture. Whisk or mix in the schnapps and 2 tablespoons of the sugar mixture. Taste and add the remaining sugar mixture, if desired. Set aside for later use.

Place the egg whites in a mixing bowl. Using clean beaters for the electric mixer, beat until foamy. Sprinkle the remaining ¼ cup sugar evenly over the top. Beat on high speed to create a soft meringue. Fold the meringue into the chocolate mixture. Place mixture in a pastry tube and squeeze into stemmed wine or compote glasses. Sprinkle with caribe and chill. Can be served warm or chilled.

Cooking Time: 10 minutes, Yield: 4 servings

PER SERVING:
Calories 330
Protein 5 g
Carbohydrates 43 g
Fiber 2 g
Fat 15 g
Saturated Fat 9 g
Cholesterol 17 mg
Sodium 44 mg

Pumpkin Pudding

This dessert has all the goodness of pumpkin pie without the crust. Sprinkling the pie with chile definitely sets it apart and actually enhances the flavor. 🌶

2 cups puréed sweet pumpkin (1 15-ounce can)

1 ½ cups evaporated skim milk

1 large egg, plus 1 egg white

½ cup firmly packed light brown sugar

2 teaspoons pumpkin pie spice or ⅓ teaspoon each ground ginger, nutmeg, allspice, and cloves

1 teaspoon ground hot chile

In a blender combine the pumpkin, milk, egg, egg white, brown sugar, and spice. Process to blend well. Pour the mixture into 6 to 8 individual buttered baking dishes.

Place in the microwave oven and cook on high for 5 minutes (see Note), or until a table knife inserted in the center comes out clean. Cook for another minute or two, if needed. Sprinkle with the chile. Serve warm.

Note: Or preheat conventional oven to 350 degrees F. Place the pudding dishes in a baking pan large enough to hold them. Add hot water to about halfway up the sides of the baking dishes. Place the pan in the oven and bake for 30 to 40 minutes, until a knife inserted in the center comes out clean.

Cooking Time: 5 to 7 minutes in a microwave oven, 30 to 40 minutes in a conventional oven, Yield: 6 to 8 servings

PER SERVING:
(1/8 recipe)
Calories 157
Protein 5 g
Carbohydrates 33 g
Fiber 4 g
Fat 1 g
Saturated Fat 0 g
Cholesterol 28 mg
Sodium 186 mg

Real Women Bios

GLORIA AGUIÑAGO and LISA AGUIÑAGO-MANSFIELD (page 14) are a mother and daughter team whose love for chile is what brought them together at their restaurant, Café Olé. Cooking from *el corazón* for fifteen years and still going strong, they continue to fight for the renaissance of the once undesirable, yet trendy, Red Light District on their beloved south side.

BETH CLAXTON (page 17) is a board certified Obstetrician and Gynecologist who enhances her practice by offering complementary alternatives to traditional western medicine. Her first love is third-world medicine having practiced in Fiji, Mexico, and Zimbabwe. Her free time is filled with cooking and yoga practice. She lives in Flagstaff, Arizona, with her husband and two daughters, Eliza and Meg.

KRISTEN DAVENPORT (page 27) is an accomplished writer and garlic farmer living in the Sangre de Cristo Mountains outside of Taos, New Mexico. She has three children, three dogs, some goats, too many chickens, Velveteen rabbits, and a good curly-haired husband to help with all the work.

DARCY FALK (page 23) makes exceptional, original artworks from recycled and hand-dyed fabrics. Her stitched textile collages are regularly shown in galleries across the U.S. In addition to creating commissioned artworks for private and corporate clients, she writes about art and life from her studio in the Southwest. Her posole is widely acclaimed.

ANGELA HAWSE (page 3) is an AMGA Certified Rock Guide, Himalayan Alpinist, and Sponsored Athlete. She has led more than twenty high-altitude expeditions, including the First Disabled Ascent of Mt. Everest in 1998. She is dedicated to conserving the mountains she loves to climb, leading many garbage clean ups and fundraising efforts. Whenever she can, Angela goes climbing near her home in Colorado with her dog, Chile.

DARA MARKS-MARINO (page 11) was a third grade teacher who switched to professional mountain bike racing after she realized that was her true passion. She lives in Arizona and has been a professional cyclist for six years with the help of her supportive husband. When she is not on her bike, she enjoys cooking, reading, running, and playing with her dog.

SARA MOULTON (page 20) is the chef of the executive dining room at *Gourmet* magazine, the food editor for ABC-TV's *Good Morning America*, and the host of *Sara's Secrets* on the Food Network. Her culinary experience includes work with Julia Child and an apprenticeship with a master chef in France. She co-founded the New York Women's Culinary Alliance, is the author of two cookbooks, and has been a regular on the Food Network for eight years.

BARBARA RICHARDSON (page 4) is the First Lady of New Mexico. Her areas of interest and work include literacy, domestic violence, childhood immunization, and the arts. She has been instrumental in bettering the lives of New Mexican children both through her position as Chair of Read Across America in New Mexico and of Big Brothers/Big Sisters First Lady's Bowl for Kids Sake.

BETHANNE GUERTIN SALLY (page 24) is a bilingual elementary school teacher in the San Francisco Bay Area. She widely incorporates chiles in her curriculum. She has traveled by bicycle through New England, by Eurorail through Europe, and she lived in Duran, Ecuador for one year. In her free time she enjoys hiking with her husband, spending time with family, and curling up with a good book.

The "Salsitas" (page 7). After creating *Secrets of Salsa: A Bilingual Cookbook by the Mexican Women of Anderson Valley* in an ESL class project, the Salsitas, as they later named themselves, experienced a personal and civic empowerment that has precipitated many a salsa tasting/booksigning event, invitations to speak, and a documentary film by two local professional filmmakers. For additional information visit: www.secretsofsalsa.com.

THE SALSITAS:

LAURA MORALES was born on a small ranch called Timbiriche in Michoacan, Mexico. She came to the United States four years ago and is very thankful because she has work here, which helps her buy food and clothes for her three children. She misses her mom and the fresh mangoes back home.

MARIA ELENA PLANCARTE loves to prepare and eat salsa of all kinds, but her most favorites are Five Green and Mango with Cucumber. She is fascinated by how interested people are in the Mexican salsas. She has one child and came here from Jacona in Michoacan, Mexico, ten years ago.

EVANGELINA ANGULO grew up in Mexico City and was married when she was sixteen years old. The oldest of her four children is now in college. She has lived here for seventeen years and really appreciates coming to school to learn English and civic skills.

SUSAN WELSAND, The Chile Woman, (page 12) started growing unique chiles twelve years ago for herself. Now a full-time grower of an endless variety of chiles, as well as bedding and potted plants, she feels blessed to work in such a soul-satisfying environment. She is dedicated to sustainability and keeping heirloom varieties of chiles available. She is currently growing around 1,100 varieties of chiles. She lives in a community full of organic growers in Indiana, and will soon be adopting a child from Guatemala.